THERAPY OUTCOME MEASURES FOR REHABILITATION PROFESSIONALS

THERAPY OUTCOME MEASURES FOR REHABILITATION PROFESSIONALS

SPEECH AND LANGUAGE THERAPY; PHYSIOTHERAPY; OCCUPATIONAL THERAPY; REHABILITATION NURSING; HEARING THERAPISTS

Second Edition

Pamela Enderby

with

Alexandra John

&

Brian Petheram

Compatible with ICF and incorporating ICD10

John Wiley & Sons, Ltd

Published 2006 John Wiley & Sons Ltd, The Atrium, Southern Gate, Chichester,
West Sussex PO19 8SQ, England

Telephone (+44) 1243 779777

Email (for orders and customer service enquiries): cs-books@wiley.co.uk
Visit our Home Page on www.wiley.com

Other Wiley Editorial Offices

John Wiley & Sons Inc., 111 River Street, Hoboken, NJ 07030, USA

Jossey-Bass, 989 Market Street, San Francisco, CA 94103-1741, USA

Wiley-VCH Verlag GmbH, Boschstr. 12, D-69469 Weinheim, Germany

John Wiley & Sons Australia Ltd, 42 McDougall Street, Milton, Queensland 4064, Australia

John Wiley & Sons (Asia) Pte Ltd, 2 Clementi Loop #02-01, Jin Xing Distripark, Singapore 129809

John Wiley & Sons Canada Ltd, 6045 Freemont Blvd, Mississauga, ONT, L5R 4J3, Canada

Wiley also publishes its books in a variety of electronic formats. Some content that appears in print may not be available in electronic books.

Library of Congress Cataloging-in-Publication Data:

Enderby, Pamela M. (Pamela Mary), 1949-
Therapy outcome measures for rehabilitation professionals : speech and language therapy, physiotherapy, occupational therapy, rehabilitation nursing, hearing therapists / Pamela Enderby ; with Alexandra John & Brian Petheram.–2nd ed.
p. ; cm.
Rev. ed. of: Therapy outcome measures manual / Pam Enderby ; with Alexandra John and Brian Petheram. San Diego : Singular Pub. Group, c1998.
Includes bibliographical references.
ISBN-13: 978-0-470-02621-2 (pbk. : alk. paper)
ISBN-10: 0-470-02621-9 (pbk. : alk. paper)
1. Medical rehabilitation–Evaluation–Handbooks, manuals, etc.
2. Outcome assessment (Medical care)–Handbooks, manuals, etc.
I. John, Alexandra. II. Petheram, Brian. III. Enderby, Pamela M. (Pamela Mary), 1949- . Therapy outcome measures manual. IV. Title.
[DNLM: 1. Outcome Assessment (Health Care)–methods–Handbooks. 2. Physical Therapy Modalities–Handbooks. 3. Disability Evaluation--Handbooks. 4. Language Therapy–methods–Handbooks. 5. Occupational Therapy–methods–Handbooks. 6. Rehabilitation Nursing–methods–Handbooks. 7. Speech Therapy–methods–Handbooks. WB 39 E57ta 2006]
RM930.E53 2006
615.8′2–dc22

2006011281

British Library Cataloguing in Publication Data

A catalogue record for this book is available from the British Library

ISBN-13: 978-0-470-02621-2
ISBN-10: 0-470-02621-9

Typeset in 12/14pt Minion by Laserwords Private Limited, Chennai, India
Printed and bound in Great Britain by Antony Rowe Ltd, Chippenham, Wiltshire
This book is printed on acid-free paper responsibly manufactured from sustainable forestry in which at least two trees are planted for each one used for paper production.

CONTENTS

PREFACE

The Therapy Outcome Measure (TOM) allows therapists to describe the relative abilities and difficulties of a patient/client in the four domains of impairment, activity, participation and well-being in order to monitor changes over time. This approach has been rigorously tested for reliability and clinical validity and can be used by physiotherapists, occupational therapists, speech and language therapists, rehabilitation nurses and hearing therapists. It aims to be quick and simple to use, taking just a few minutes to complete and has been used for treatment planning, clinical management, audit, and research. It allows for the aggregation of data so that comparisons can be made for the purposes of internal and external benchmarking. The approach has been trialed in order to establish the differential outcomes between different client groups and different rehabilitation units.

SECTION 1

Theoretical Underpinning and Testing

INTRODUCTION

This manual is intended to assist with the practical implementation of gathering outcome data on patients/clients receiving treatment.

The data related to the development of this approach, the reliability and validity trials, the development of the scales, and the pilot study results are reported in the accompanying technical report. It is essential that, prior to implementing this method of measuring outcome, a thorough understanding of the philosophical and technical underpinning is achieved.

Over the last decade, there has been a growing awareness of the importance of being able to gather information that could assist in identifying specific gains related to treatment programmes. This should not only help to identify areas for resource change but also enable health care professionals to monitor the effectiveness of their treatments with individual clients.

One of the essential components of this approach is the acknowledgement that therapy endeavours to have an impact on many areas of the client's life. Traditionally, most assessments of patients/clients have concentrated on changes in the deficit/disorder, whereas goals of therapy might also aim to alter the functional components of communication, mobility, activities of daily living (ADL), autonomy, coping skills and adaptation. In order to determine if we are being effective with different client groups, it is necessary that we have a good understanding of the patient's/client's situation prior to, during and following the treatment.

Outcomes have been defined as results or visible effects of interventions. In healthcare, outcomes form part of the quality cycle which can be improved through evaluation. Outcome data can provide information on the impact of interventions, to identify the effectiveness of practices (care pathways, costs of care, resources), and facilitate the design of guidelines (Shaw and Miller, 2000; The College of Speech and Language Therapists, 1991). Information from a number of sources is required in order to build a picture of the outcome of current practice, and to identify the evidence for best practice. By understanding discrepancies between the two, issues for change can be identified, changes effected, and quality of care improved.

Quality assurance requires the health worker to provide a high standard of practice, yet definitions of quality in respect of its application to the provision of healthcare remain ambiguous. The UK Government White Paper (1999) defined quality as providing an equitable, efficient and responsive service, as follows:

- ***Equity***: to reduce variation in health by targeting need;
- ***Efficiency***: effective care for best use of money; and

- ***Responsiveness:*** to meet individual needs while responsive to changes in circumstances and knowledge.

Clinical governance has been introduced to the National Health Service in the United Kingdom as a means of ensuring quality (White Paper Department of Health, 1999). As a concept, clinical governance provides a framework to ensure quality of clinical care, so that service users benefit through continued endeavours for improvement (Buetow and Roland, 1999). The five areas needed to be addressed in order to achieve this quality improvement are: good use of information (with education, patient/client liaison and multi-disciplinary involvement); reduction of inequity and variations in care; involvement of individuals in service and care plans; sharing good practice (learning by comparison, benchmarking); and detecting and dealing with poor performance (Swage, 2000 pp. 48–49).

The evaluation of outcomes is an important part of clinical governance. Outcome data can provide a baseline of current practice, against which comparisons over time or with other similar services can be made in order to identify useful information on practice. If the data is to inform change, it is essential that it is seen to be relevant as well as being accessible to stakeholders. The use of any outcome indicators requires those using the method to be trained to use it reliably as well as appreciating its clinical relevance.

Recent radical changes in health service delivery have increased the pressure on all service providers to examine their methods for reporting results relating to the impact of health services (Wilkin et al. 1992). There is greater awareness of the disparity of health care, widely differing costs and concerns about demonstrable effectiveness. Information reflecting the effects of treatment is essential in order to modify methods of provision, influence purchasing patterns and assist in monitoring contracts along with harnessing efforts to improve care (Ware, 1991; Ware and Sherbourne, 1992). Hence, professionals are becoming more conscious of their social as well as clinical responsibility to account for the value and benefits of interventions.

The importance of basing health care on a firm knowledge base to improve cost-effectiveness and efficiency is highly laudable. However, moving towards gathering information in a formal and reliable way that will clarify health gain is a complex process. There has been a tendency in collecting data to focus on input, throughput and output, to equate the outcome of an activity with the rate at which patients/clients are being referred or discharged rather than determining the impact of particular care packages on an individual's health (Hopkins, 1993).

"Purchasers are not indifferent to the question of quality but they are stymied by the 'current state of the art' in quality measurement" (Health Care Advisory Board, 1994, p. 32); this is due both to clinical and technological limitations and different views regarding what constitutes quality. Replicable and meaningful data are hard to find and even harder to decipher.

Outcome measurement is complex because it is difficult to define the effects of care, and frequently there is little agreement regarding what health programs are endeavouring to achieve with different client groups. For example, with a patients/client with progressive neurological disease, it may be more appropriate for a clinician to be concerned with appropriate pain management and the assurance that death is going to be handled appropriately rather than with a "cure".

Most outcome measures have concentrated on negative outcomes, such as the reduction of morbidity and mortality, and have failed to reflect the quality of care received by the majority of patients/clients who are influenced positively by their treatment. Further difficulties arise when one examines the complexity of what health services try to deliver. Health care programmes frequently include aspects such as prevention of disease, information for patients/clients and relatives and supporting, counselling and managing secondary complications. Thus, the measures of outcome that are used currently may be seen as reflecting a simplistic view of the aims of the health intervention.

Informing investment for health care on objective evidence has led to a greater reliance on published research. In most medical and rehabilitation fields, there is a limited amount of conclusive research that can be used alone to inform practice. Frequently, research attracts specific cohorts of patients/clients that do not reflect the range of difficulties requiring health service involvement in a wide range of settings. Furthermore, although research is essential, purchasers and managers have difficulty using research as a benchmark for their own practices if there are no methods to continually monitor the performance of patients/clients within localities on a regular basis for comparative purposes. The Cochrane Systematic Reviews, Evidence Based Medicine Reviews, Database of Abstracts of Reviews of Effects and the OT Seeker – Occupational Therapy Systematic Review of Evidence – have been developed to provide a ready source of quality research applicable to effectiveness of care.

Many health status/outcome and assessment scales purport to provide objective data on populations and specific subgroups. Donovan et al. (1993) gave an overview of health status measures divided into six categories:

1. ***General health measures.*** These provide global profiles of health, including well-being, function and social and emotional health (e.g. General Health Questionnaire (Goldberg, 1992), Nottingham Health Profile (Hunt and McEven, 1980), Medical Outcomes Study Instrument SF36 (Reisenberg and Glass, 1989)).
2. ***Measures of physical function.*** These reflect the level of physical impairment and disability within general populations (e.g. Lambeth Disability Screening Questionnaire (Patrick et al. 1981)), or for specific groups (e.g. a unified ADL evaluation form (Donaldson et al. 1973)). These assess functions such as dressing, mobility and self-care.

3. ***Pain measures.*** These are instruments that are generally used with specific client groups and reflect the intensity/duration of pain (e.g. MeGill Pain Questionnaire (Melzack, 1983), the Visual Analogue Scale (Scott and Huskisson, 1979)).
4. ***Social health measures.*** The Social Health Battery (Williams et al. 1981) and similar batteries assess the strength of people's social support mechanisms and networks.
5. ***Quality of life measures.*** The Four Single Items of Well-being (Andrews and Crandall, 1976) and the Quality of Life Index (Spitzer et al. 1981) measure the elusive "satisfaction of individuals with life".
6. ***Specific disease measures.*** These measures assess issues relevant to particular client groups in order to establish the impact and/or severity of conditions (e.g. the Arthritis Impact Measurement Scale (Meenan et al. 1980), The Frenchay Dysarthria Assessment (Enderby, 1981)).

These are a few of the plethora of different tools and approaches used to monitor the performance of patients/clients who have different diseases/health difficulties and who are receiving input from numerous health professionals. However, collecting, pooling and comparing these data are difficult and end up being less than informative for those who wish to make decisions. Traditional clinical indicators used in health research and outcome measurement have several major shortcomings: they tend to focus on rare negative outcomes and omit the degrees of benefit of certain treatments. Furthermore, other traditional measures focus on biological outcomes, for example, reductions in spasticity, infections or amputations. It is well known that health is considerably more to an individual than the reduction of disease alone. "Health is a slippery concept (Anderson et al. 1990, p. 205), a complex combination of lack of illness, well-being, control over life, and autonomy".

Despite considerable work on devising and validating impairment scales (Ebrahim et al. 1985; Wade, 1992), their use in the clinic and in clinical trials has sometimes failed to reflect improvement where clinical judgement and other evidence suggests that therapy has been beneficial (Harewood et al. 1994). Most studies on the efficacy of different nursing and therapy professions have used measures of impairment: for example, the accuracy of articulation, muscle power or range of movement. However, examination of what nursing and therapy try to achieve demonstrates that modifying impairment is only one component of the therapeutic target (Enderby, 1992). Thus, the primary goal of health care for many patients/clients, particularly those with long-term chronic conditions, is to maximise function in everyday life and to achieve the highest level of well-being (Stewart et al. 1989; Austin and Clark, 1993; Sarno, 1993).

The work presented here was stimulated by the desire to have a single, simple measure that would reflect the status of an individual more broadly than is possible with other assessment procedures: the degree of "disorder" (i.e. impairment), the everyday limitations in function (i.e. activity) and the social consequences (i.e. participation). Previously, therapists had to turn to different tools if they wished to assess the patient/client holistically. This often caused difficulties because the various tools were not designed to dovetail and might give different weightings to different components.

The starting point of outcome measurement should be a greater understanding about what is to be achieved within a health care program. There is a need for multidimensional outcome measures in order that the effect of different health services in all aspects of management can be reflected. Assessment of treatment outcomes is complicated by the multiplicity of objectives in most treatment programmes that are not readily measured, as they involve goals other than those assessed by the standard procedures for assessing impairment.

Health service authorities have been charged with the responsibility of purchasing a pattern of health care provisions that accords with the needs of the local population (Department of Health, 1989, 1999a, 1999b). This stimulated a resurgence of interest in surveying population needs along with the effort to establish effectiveness of services. The measures outlined by Donovan et al. (1993) have occasionally been used to survey health needs as well as to measure effectiveness. However, most measures were originally designed for one or the other purpose and do not necessarily transfer readily. Even when contained in the field of establishing health needs, Donovan et al. argued that they may be less effective than hoped, as the level of generalisable characteristics of health status measures makes their interpretation difficult and possibly inadequate to support purchasing decisions, as it is not possible to map general measures of pain, mobility or distress to the requirements for specific services. We would suggest that this places an even higher demand on the need for service outcome data.

In most specialities there are wide variations in clinical practice, with limited agreement as to the most effective treatment, limited criteria to indicate the appropriate level, type or amount of intervention and a lack of information that the intervention itself is justified. The small amount of research in some fields fuels only debate, rather than giving answers that would help to define the best practice. Thus, there is a continued tendency to equate the outcome of activity with process measures, such as throughput and activity levels, rather than determining the effect of the care package in its totality, which is the aim of collecting information on outcomes as presented here (Øvretveit 1992, 1998).

WORLD HEALTH ORGANISATION CLASSIFICATION

World Health Organisation International Classification of Impairment, Disability and Handicap (WHO ICIDH) (World Health Organisation, 1980) reflected the concept that health problems impact on many areas of an individual's life, and this classification made explicit that medical conditions produce multiple difficulties for the individual and any outcome measure must reflect these different areas. The realisation that health care systems were attempting to have a broader impact than the reduction and prevention of disease alone necessitated the development of a language that could capture an extension to the sequence of events underlying illness-related phenomena. Wood and Badley (1978) and Wood (1980) suggested the following profile:

Disease → Impairment → Disability → Handicap.

A problem at the level of the organ could result in an impairment, which caused a disability, which impacted on the individual's life resulting in a handicap.

Each dimension can be summarised as follows:

• Impairment	Dysfunction resulting from pathological changes in system.
• Disability	Consequence of impairment in terms of functional performance (disturbance at the level of person).
• Handicap	Disadvantages experienced by the individual as a result of impairment and disabilities. It reflects interaction with an adaptation to the individual's surroundings.

This form of classification allowed one to reflect on the different impacts on the health of an individual. For example, some conditions will "impair" slightly but cause severe "disability" and "handicap", whereas others may show major "impairment" but limited "disability" and "handicap".

However, studies have indicated poor correlations between the impairments, disabilities and handicaps in some individuals from particular client groups. For example, in heart failure there may be no relation between cardiac output (impairment) with treadmill-exercise tolerance, timed walking tests (disabilities), and social activity (handicap) (Cowley et al. 1991). This lack of direct relationship between impairment, disability and handicap also applies in chronic airway disease (Williams and Bury, 1989). From the patient's/client's point of view, impairment may be of less importance than the restrictions placed on everyday life. The following case histories (Tables 1-1

Table 1-1. CASE STUDY 1: Mr K.

Impairment	Mr K has a mild expressive and receptive language disorder, dysphasia/aphasia.
Disability/activity	Although he speaks quite freely, he has difficulty making himself understood quickly in a group of people and has stopped using the telephone. Mr K occasionally misunderstands meanings, particularly if there is a rapid change of subject. He is dependant on others being attentive and patient/client listeners.
Handicap/participation	Mr K is now unable to be employed as he had been previously, has withdrawn from social situations, has given up all hobbies, and no longer contributes to decision-making.
Summary	This gentleman could be seen as having a mild impairment, a moderate limitation in the activity of communication and quite a severe social disadvantage.

Table 1-2. CASE STUDY 2: Mr SP.

Impairment	Mr SP has had a stroke, has a mild hemiplegia with some loss of dexterity in his left hand and has increased tone in his left leg.
Disability/activity	Mr SP is able to undertake all tasks for himself but prefers his wife to help him with most activities, and he requires extra time and encouragement in all ADL.
Handicap/participation	Mr SP has lost confidence and no longer makes decisions on finance or social matters, and his wife has taken over all household and social tasks. He has retired early and withdrawn from previously enjoyed social activities.
Summary	This gentleman has a mild/moderate motor impairment. His performance in daily activities or in social participation matches his capabilities.

and 1-2) illustrate the impact of a cerebral vascular disease on different individuals and how, from the individual's point of view, impairment may be of less importance than the restrictions these place on everyday life.

Since Wood and Badley's work in 1978 and Wood's in 1980, there has been considerable discussion with regard to the aspect of emotional distress/well-being associated with disease and dysfunction. While the ICIDH acknowledges the impact on a person's well-being, the emotional consequences were not included in the classification. We found in the study of therapy goals (Enderby and John, 1997) that frequently there were goals associated with improving the emotional status of the patient/client and relatives, and therefore in an early stage of our work we decided that this dimension has to be identified separately. After all, if a rehabilitation programme for a severely disabled person is focussed on improving their adjustment and coping strategies, it is important to be able to identify the impact of this intervention.

INTERNATIONAL CLASSIFICATION OF FUNCTIONING

A revision of the ICIDH was undertaken by the WHO coordinated by the WCC WHO Collaborating Centre in the Netherlands and resulted in the production of the WHO's International Classification of Functioning, Disability, and Health (World Health Organisation, 2001) (ICF). The revised classifications correspond with the original three dimensions of the ICIDH with the addition of environmental impact on the individual and personal factors. The ICIDH dimensions have been renamed following consultation with users.

The International Classification of Functioning (ICF) organises the classification system in two parts. Part 1 classifies functioning and disability and Part 2 deals with contextual factors. Functioning and disability in Part 1 includes the dimensions of body systems and body structure and activity and participation (BAP) denoting functioning from an individual perspective and that of their society. Figure 1-1 illustrates the interactions between the different dimensions of ICF.

The dimension of impairment is renamed body and related to body functions and structures (*impairments*); disability is renamed activity (*limitations*), while handicap is renamed participation (*restrictions*). This more positive terminology is favoured by many disability groups and moves the classification from a medical to a more social model. ICF has now two parts. Part 1 concerns functioning and disability while Part 2 concerns the contextual factors of environment and personal factors. Table 1-3 shows an overview of the ICF. The ICF has components which can be viewed as positive or negative, each component consists of domains which are units of classification. Thus, health and health related states can be recorded by selecting a category code and

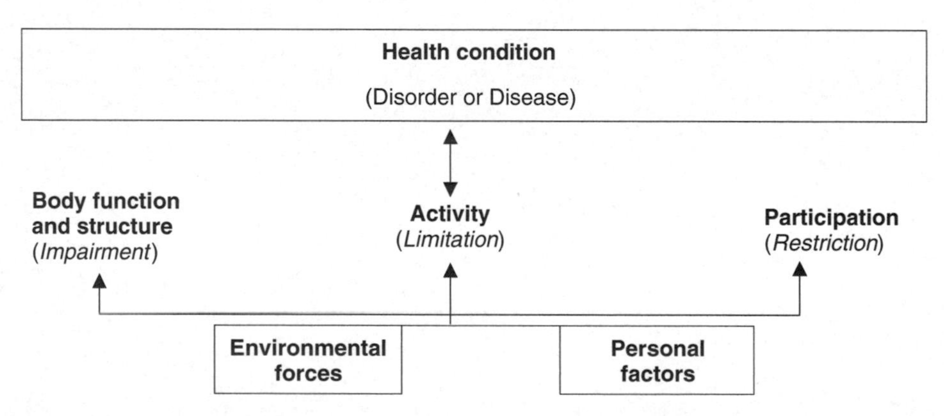

Figure 1-1. Interactions between the dimensions of ICF Parts 1 and 2 (WHO-ICF 2001).

Table 1-3. An overview of ICF.

	Part 1: Functioning and Disability		Part 2: Contextual Factors	
Components	Body Functions and Structures	Activities and Participation	Environmental Factors	Personal Factors
Domains	**Body functions:** physiological and psychological functions of body systems **Body structures:** anatomical parts of body	Life areas (tasks, actions)	External influences on functioning and disability	Internal influences of functioning and disability
Constructs	Change in body functions (physiological) Change in body structure (anatomical)	*Capacity* Executing a task in a normal environment *Performance* Executing tasks in current environment	Facilitating or hindering	Impact of attributes of the person
Positive aspect	Functional and structural integrity	Activities participation	Facilitators	N/A
	Functioning			
Negative aspect	**Impairments:** problems in body function or structure as a significant deviation or loss	**Activity** *Limitation:* difficulties an individual may have in executing activities **Participation** *Restrictions:* problems an individual may experience in involvement in life situations	Barriers/ hindrances	N/A
	Disability			

Table 1-4. ICF components.

Body Structures and Functions	Activities and Participation	Environmental Factors
Mental functions Voice and speech functions Sensory and pain functions Skin and related functions Neuromuscular and movement related functions Cardiovascular, haematological and respiratory systems Genitourinary and reproductive functions Digestive, metabolic and endocrine systems	Learning and applying knowledge General tasks and demands Communication Movement Self-care Domestic life areas Interpersonal interactions Major life areas Community, social and civic life	Products and technology Natural environment and human-made changes to environment Support and relationships Attitudes Services, systems and policies

adding qualifiers. Qualifiers are number codes that state the extent of the functioning or disability or environmental factor (as a facilitator or barrier).

The change from ICIDH to ICF places the constructs which underpin the therapy outcome measure (TOM) in Part 1, "Functioning and Disability", and the TOM rating scales aim to capture the impact of the impairment, activity and participation experienced by the individual which are described under the "Negative Aspect" of the ICF. These factors affect the well-being of the individual, and well-being is defined as the level of distress or upset experienced as a result of the limitations and difficulties encountered. The importance of addressing the emotional state in health care delivery was identified three decades ago by Rosser (1976) who suggested this as an outcome measurement. Subsequent studies have found that well-being is an important factor in noting significant clinical change (Gamiats et al. (1992); Long (1996); Paterson (1996)).

This approach permits therapists to organise patient/client information so that areas of difficulty can be classified into the different ICF components. Table 1-4 shows the ICF model of this grouping.

The language used by professionals when assisting those with different health difficulties is diverse. Even within a profession, descriptions of disorders, treatment methods and goals may be phrased in such different ways that communication is made difficult. The use of ICF allows therapists to communicate more effectively among themselves and with their managers. It also facilitates reflection of the different domains of treatment according to the different client groups served. For example, the emphasis of speech and language therapy for a person with organic voice or phonological disorder may be impairment reduction, whereas with other client groups, such as adult learning disability, the emphasis of therapy may be the reduction of social barriers. While the emphasis in occupational therapy for a person with motor difficulties may be on limitations in performance affecting ADL or in physiotherapy to improve or remediate the underlying impairment, for example, by treating impaired muscle tone, the nurse may address blood pressure, daily activities or social integration.

Despite high level, philosophically informed, international debate, there will probably never be a totally acceptable model of disability. The medical model and the social model have their places and offer components that facilitate the understanding of the needs of disabled people at different times. Therapists do not necessarily feel entirely comfortable with either, as they are aware that "illness", "disease" or "dysfunction" is a psychophysiological process that limits the person's coping abilities (Fugl-Meyer et al. 1991). This philosophy is core to one of the aims of rehabilitation, which is to mobilise the resources of an individual so that, by having realistic goals and adapting physically and psychologically, they may achieve optimal life satisfaction. This approach is supported by McCrae and Costa (1986) who found that subjects who used effective coping strategies reported higher subsequent life satisfaction. These authors, along with many others (e.g. Stephen and Hetu, 1992; Whiteneck et al. 1992; Frattali, 1991), support the classification of impairment, disability and handicap as one that can reflect the complexity of the challenges in rehabilitation, but we suggest the addition of the concept of distress/well-being in its own right rather than being embedded within the other domains.

From the patient/client point of view, impairment may be of less importance than the restrictions these place on everyday life. There has been an increasing clamour for the development of functional assessments, and some authors have even called for deficit measures (impairment) to be abandoned, particularly when evaluating rehabilitation (Blomert, 1990; Haley et al. 1991). It is probably more appropriate to call for the field to be redressed and balanced, adding methods to reflect the impact of functional, and social and emotional aspects to that of the impairment. The ICF gives equal emphasis to each dimension, likewise, the TOM is based on the belief that each domain is important, and should be given equal weight, so that the client's individual circumstances are considered. This reflects how therapists are trained to approach rehabilitation (Wade, 1992).

Investigating Whether the WHO Classification is Useful in Identifying Therapy Goals

A study of outcome measurement essentially must start by having a full understanding of what a particular service is trying to achieve. This can then act as the benchmark to determine whether the stated goals have been achieved. Therapy aims to:

- ***Improve/remediate*:** the underlying impairment to cognition, structure and physiology. Speech and language therapy (SLT) example: impaired communication evidenced in auditory attention deficits, voice, phonological, syntactic, semantic, pragmatic, motor or sensory disorders. Physiotherapy/occupational therapy (PT/OT) example: impaired muscle tone, range of movement, balance, cognitive, motor or sensory disorders and alleviation of pressure areas.
- ***Extend functional activity relating to performance*:** SLT example: communicating ideas, relating stories, by teaching signing systems, use of communication aids, or facilitating intelligibility. PT/OT example: by encouraging adapted methods in the ADL or by increasing independence by introducing and encouraging the appropriate use of environmental aids and appliances.
- ***Develop strategies to accommodate the personal social disadvantage of the deficit*:** SLT example: modifying attitudes and providing strategies for teachers, patients/clients and caregivers, attending a social events, sustaining work role. PT/OT example: working with employers and clients to assist return to work.
- ***Support the patient/client and caregivers during the adjustment phase*:** Example: identify upset or concern, provide counselling, encouragement and support.

The first edition of the TOM (Enderby, 1992) was underpinned by an investigation to establish whether the WHO (ICIDH) classification would be appropriate for consideration for development as a model for outcomes, and the case notes from 300 persons receiving therapy were examined. The goals in these notes were identified and a large majority could be included under the groupings of body/impairment, activity and participation. **There were no client groups that did not have goals attributed to all of these sections.** One group of goals identified by therapists, relating to the emotional well-being of clients and their families, was difficult to mesh with this original classification. Therapists and nurses frequently noted attempts to reduce anxiety, depression, anger and fear and to improve emotional control and coping strategies. As so many goals were identified in this area, it was felt important to extend the classification by adding the heading of **"Well-being"** as a dimension.

Many treatises on the effectiveness of health service provision, rehabilitation and outcome dwell on the importance of "quality of life". Although this term has become increasingly fashionable, it has not been defined (McKenna et al. 1993; Wade, 2003). Therapists feel strongly that they contribute to improving this elusive "*je ne sais quoi*", but in developing these measures we have avoided the use of the term "quality of life" because it lacks specificity and means different things to different people. However, the essentials of this concept are probably captured in the domains of handicap/participation and distress/well-being. Interestingly, no goals specifying "improving quality of life" were found in the case notes but goals to do with "improving self esteem" and "improving personal autonomy [handicaps/participation]", "teaching coping strategies to reduce fear", and "helping the person to come to terms with [distress]" were mentioned frequently.

The following two case histories illustrate the different balances of the effect of different disorders (Tables 1-5, 1-6).

Table 1-5. CASE STUDY 1: Mrs PR.

Impairment	Mrs PR has had multiple sclerosis for 15 years. She is severely ataxic and has increased tone in all limbs. Her sitting balance is poor.
Disability/activity	Mrs PR uses an adapted wheelchair and all aids and appliances in the home effectively. She is in an adapted accommodation and can get to the local shops. She is able to care for the house, provide meals for the family and communicate effectively.
Handicap/participation	Mrs PR plays an active social role, she is a school governor as well as acting on the local community health council. She enjoys her garden and wheelchair dancing.
Well-being/distress	Mrs PR is a determined, resourceful lady who, not surprisingly, becomes concerned and frustrated on some occasions, but is generally positive and uses good emotional support strategies.
Summary	Mrs PR has a severe level of impairment but overcomes most functional restrictions using resourcefulness and appropriate aids. Thus, she is only partially limited in activity and is not socially disadvantaged in any specific way.

Table 1-6. CASE STUDY 2: MR C.

Impairment	Mr C is a 40-year-old gentleman who has cerebral palsy resulting in a severe abnormality of tone. Mr C is quadriplegic and dysarthric.
Disability/activity	Mr C is wheelchair bound, but is totally independent, using an adapted wheelchair and living in adapted accommodation. He can communicate in all situations with a communication aid with special adaptations for the telephone.
Handicap/participation	Mr C is employed as a solicitor and is an active member in the disability movement, he has a full work and social life and his views are sought and valued by a number of contacts.
Well-being/distress	Mr C experiences occasional frustration resulting from restrictions in access and negative attitudes occasionally encountered.
Summary	This gentleman, who has a very severe level of impairment, has been able to overcome his difficulties so that functionally, while restricted, he is independent and he is not socially disadvantaged in any particular way.

DEVELOPMENT OF THE TOM

During the 1980s, Enderby (1992) began work to develop a measure of outcome for therapists that would reflect the changes effected as a result of therapy intervention. At that time, the trend in the method of measuring outcome focused on the results of standardised assessment, which measured levels of impairment or communication or of achieving treatment goals. However, while two patients/clients can achieve the same goal with therapy, they may have different outcomes. For example, treatment that focuses on teaching specific new vocabulary can improve communication skills in one person, while it may reduce frustration and facilitate social interaction in another. Thus, achieving a goal results in different outcomes for different individuals and reflects the complexities of capturing the outcomes of an intervention. A consequence of this limited approach was that other aspects of intervention, including social and emotional issues, were frequently not included in outcome measurement. Other methods of assessing the outcome of care were needed if the patient/client were to be assessed holistically.

The WHO classification of disease (World Health Organisation, 1980) provided dimensions that equated to the areas targeted in treatment. The dimensions of impairment and disability/activity were focused on clinical issues, while those of handicap/participation and the additional dimension of well-being were concerned more with the quality of life. The TOM was developed to reflect the WHO classification system (see p. 18). It was based around the body, individual and society levels, which could then be individually rated to denote the level of difficulty experienced. On the TOM, as with the WHO classification system model, a status of "normal" was defined as normal for a human being given his/her age, sex, culture, and any "difficulty" reflected the deviation from this status for that individual. There was a difference between the TOM model and that of the WHO ICIDH in that disability was not defined as a consequence of impairment or handicap as a consequence of impairment and disability. Rather, the TOM model allowed each dimension to be rated independently. The revised WHO classification system ICF (see p. 12) also views each dimension as independent but inter-related. The WHO-ICF definitions (World Health Organisation, 2001) of "Body, Activity, Participation" (BAP) are summarised in Table 1-7 and can be seen to correspond with the concepts rated as three dimensions of the TOM. However, the TOM encapsulates the individual in life situations along with environmental factors in the dimension of participation.

Table 1-7. WHO-ICF BAP descriptions.

Attribute	Body Functions and Structures	Activities	Participation	Contextual Factors
Level of functioning	Body (body parts)	Individual (person as a whole)	Society (life situations)	Environmental factors (external influence on functioning) and personal factors (internal influence on functioning)
Characteristics	Function/ structure	Performance of activities	Involvement in life situations	Features of the individual's world and individual's attitude
Aspects	Impairment: functional/ structural	Activity: limitation	Participation: restriction	Facilitators, barriers, hindrances

TOM Model

The TOM dimensions originated from the dimensions of WHO ICDH and corresponds with the ICF. The TOM is a professionally and operationally defined scale and considers specific concepts, namely:

Impairment is concerned with the integrity of body systems, and includes psychological and physiological structures and functioning. It reflects the degree of abnormality observed, in terms of its variance from the norm for a human being (of same age, gender etc.).

Activity/Disability is concerned with the limitations on actions or functions for an individual, given his/her abilities/disabilities.

Participation/Handicap is concerned with the disadvantage experienced by the individual, reflecting circumstances, social participation, interaction and autonomy.

Well-being/Distress is concerned with emotions, feelings, burden of upset, concern and anxiety and level of satisfaction with the condition.

The concepts judged in each TOM dimension are illustrated in the Figure 1-2.

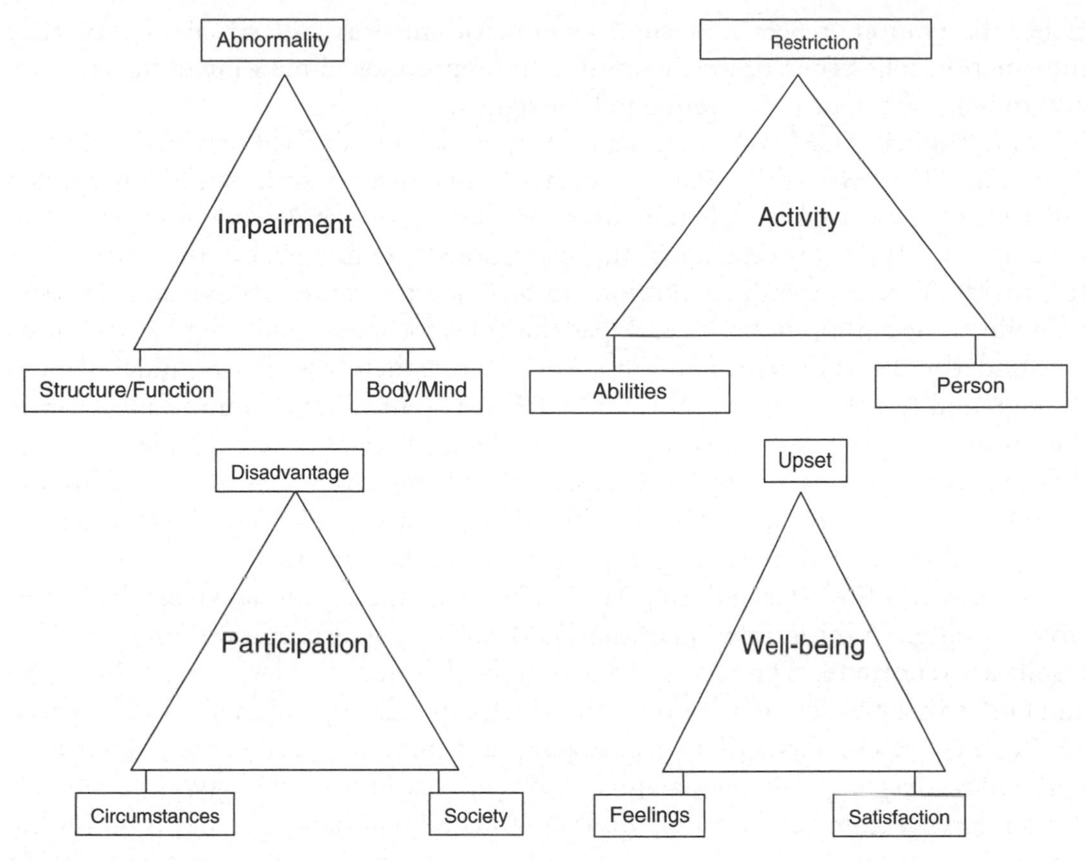

Figure 1-2. TOM dimensions.

Each of the four TOM dimensions (impairment, activity, participation and well-being) is rated on a six-point ordinal rating scale, with 0 representing the severe end of the scale and 5 representing normal for a human being given age, sex and culture. The integers are defined with a semantic operational code that identifies the severity of the difficulty experienced on each dimension allowing the assessor to indicate whether the person is slightly better or worse than the descriptor, resulting in an 5-point scale and undefined half-points providing an 11-point scale (Table 1-8).

The procedure for using the TOM requires the therapist to assess the individual referred for treatment using their usual assessment procedures, such as standardised

Table 1-8. TOM ordinal scale.

Profound		Severe		Severe/ Moderate		Moderate		Mild		Normal
0	0.5	1	1.5	2	2.5	3	3.5	4	4.5	5

tests, observation, report and consideration of medical and social history. The information collected leads the therapist to the appropriate dimension of the measure and to judge the appropriate rating to be assigned.

The original TOM core scale had an operationally defined severity scale (see Appendix VI). It was recognised that such a simple severity scale can be interpreted differently when used by different users. Therefore, in 1992 work was started to develop the TOM by expanding the operational definitions on the core scales to provide disorder-specific definitions to facilitate the rating of cases and increase reliability. The authors initially developed the TOM for speech and language therapists (see Enderby, 1992; Enderby and John, 1997). Subsequently work was undertaken to develop and test this approach for use by PT, OT, rehabilitation nurses and hearing therapists. Over the next six years the TOM-detailed scales were expanded to cover different client groups seen by PT, OT, speech and language therapists, rehabilitation nurses and hearing therapists. The specific client groups were selected by clinicians as representative of the main client groups seen within their services.

A study was undertaken during 1993–1994 with speech and language therapists, which resulted in the adaptation of the TOM for ten communication disorders. The results are reported in a project report and in the literature (Enderby et al. 1995; John and Enderby, 2000). The ten disorders for which expanded operational codes had been developed were: child speech language impairment, phonological disorders, dysarthria, dysfluency, dysphagia, dysphasia/aphasia, dysphonia, hearing therapy/aural rehabilitation, laryngectomy and learning disability/mental retardation (Enderby and John, 1997). The study aimed to develop expanded operational descriptors for the TOM Core Scales for each disorder, and involved 100 SLTs at eight geographical sites. The SLTs at each site independently developed operational descriptors for the disorders in their specialism. Thus the paediatric SLT team developed the descriptors for the child disorders, such as language impairment or phonological disorders, while the adult team developed the descriptors appropriate to their teams' area of expertise, such as dysphasia or voice disorders. The definitions in the specific scales aimed to achieve a method of communicating views of therapists about the severity and nature of the presentation within a domain; thus in essence they attempt to clarify what is meant by "severe, moderate, mild", and so on. The descriptors should prompt the therapist to help with "best match" and reflect their clinical judgement, that is "my patient/client is most like that". It is unlikely that any patient/client will fit precisely within any descriptor or have all the deficits or abilities represented in the scale description. Therapists, generally, unconsciously rank patients/clients, for example "he is a bit better than her", "she is the worst I have seen with this disorder", and so on. The scale attempts to make these judgements more explicit.

The TOM-adapted scale was used to rate cases and to assess the competence of the descriptors and their ability to capture the key behaviours observed in a disorder on each dimension. Therefore, through use of the Delphi technique, a set of unique descriptors emerged from the speech and language therapy teams of "experts" in their field within each site. The descriptors were then revised by the research team, who combined the wording from each set of descriptors for a disorder. The composite descriptors were then distributed to the sites for comment and ratification. Once the separate teams had agreed the wording for the operational descriptors, the TOM-adapted scales were put to trial by the clinicians. There followed a reliability trial with representatives from the teams, and a period of data collection which produced more than 1000 case results. The results of the data collection were used to assess the face validity of the data produced by the TOM as an outcome indicator for different disorder groups. This pilot study found that the TOM, with the expanded operational codes for specific disorders, was able to provide valid data on treatment outcomes that reflected change. However, this data was collected only over a short period of time and further data collection studies were conducted to test the TOM. The results of these are reported in the section "Benchmarking". The development of the occupational therapy, physiotherapy, hearing therapy and rehabilitation nursing scales followed the same methodology at later dates.

VALIDITY

For a measure to be valid, it needs to give a true and accurate value of something or a concept (Hammersley, 1987; Behi and Nolan, 1995). Validity concerns what is being measured. Whether the scale measures what one believes that it is measuring, and whether it truly measures what it says it measures rather than some related concept (Nolan and Behi, 1995; Wilkin et al. 1992). The usefulness of a measure will depend on the ability to make valid inferences from it, as the better the constructs are represented in the measure, the more reliance can be placed upon the results. Therefore, the content of a scale is important to its validity and should tap the relevant areas of interest. When the items to be measured are physical items, which can be measured objectively, then it is easier to construct a valid measure, such as when measuring volume, or degree of movement. It is harder to describe a valid measure when the construct is abstract, as it is harder to observe a variable that is not itself directly observable. However, abstract concepts can be measured indirectly by creating indicators that operationalise the concepts and permit their measurement (Hammersley, 1987; Behi and Nolan, 1995; Nolan and Behi, 1995; Wilkin et al. 1992; Streiner and Norman, 1989). This is the approach adopted by the TOM.

The development of a measure for abstract constructs involves a number of stages (Bryman, 1988). There is the development and defining of the underlying theory, or construct, to be measured; the specification of the different concepts; the selection of indicators to have observable characteristics of the concepts; and, finally, the formation of the indices so that the indicators are put into defined scales (nominal, ordinal, interval or ratio). Once this stage has been completed, the exact use of the measure has to be defined, as does the administration, the setting, with whom it will be used and how often, and who will interpret the results (Hammersley, 1987). The precision of the measure is another factor to consider, as the measure has to be precise enough to meet its purpose (Streiner and Norman, 1989). Therefore, in validating a measure, there is a need to determine the degree of confidence that can be placed on the inferences drawn from the individual's scores on that measure. In other words, can one believe what the measure indicates?

The literature describes three classic ways of ascertaining validity, namely, content, criterion and construct. Validity can be measured by ascertaining the degree to which what has been measured corresponds with other independent measures obtained by different research tools. At present, there are no comparable measures to the TOM that could be used as a "gold" standard. Therefore, it is not possible to test criterion validity, with its requirement to compare the results of the measure with another. Nor can construct validity be used because there is not, as yet, sufficient knowledge of the pattern of relationships, regarding the distribution of scores among different groups, to allow comparisons. Therefore, face and content validity are the descriptions of validity that have been addressed in developing the measure.

Face validity concerns whether, on the face of it, the measure captures the qualities to be measured. The criterion for assessing face validity rests on the subjective judgement, which is based on a review of the measure; that the selection of items appears sensible, in the view of a panel of experts. This approach to validation has been described as "validation by assumption"; that the instrument measures such and such because an expert says it does (Guildford, 1954; Hammersley, 1987; Streiner and Norman, 1989).

Content validity concerns whether the domain of content is relevant to the measure; whether the items included in the domain are representative samples of the target behaviours. Appropriate content is more likely if a number of representative judges are used to generate and select the items for the scales and if the content included is regarded as important, for example, as supported through the literature. Demonstration of content validity rests mainly on an "appeal to reason" in respect of the adequacy with which the domain has been defined.

Acceptance of the face and content validity of the TOM was based on a review by an "expert" panel, comprising therapists working within the particular specialisms covered by the measure.

The TOM comprises of four core scales, one for each dimension. In order to facilitate decision-making, and reliability of judgement, descriptions were added. These provided operational descriptions for whole points on the scale. The TOM descriptors' scales were developed by therapists specialising in different client groups, from different health districts contributing to the content of the scales through use of the Delphi technique. The differing scales developed were amalgamated to form an agreed-on "set". These were tested by therapists rating cases and assessing the competence of the descriptors and their ability to capture the key behaviours observed in a disorder on each dimension. Through this testing a set of unique descriptors emerged from the therapy teams of "experts" in their field within each site. The participating therapy teams collected TOM data on more than 1000 cases over a 6-month period. The results of this data collection were used to assess the validity of the data produced by the TOM as an outcome indicator for different disorder groups. The teams were able to compare the TOM results with their own observations on the cases in order to assess the validity of the results. The study found that the TOM, with the expanded operational codes for specific disorders, was able to provide valid data on outcomes of therapy intervention that reflected change.

Table 1-9 shows how the core scale was expanded to include descriptors for a specific client group.

Table 1-9. Core impairment scale and dysphasia impairment descriptors.

Core Scale Impairment	Description for Dysphasia
0 The most severe presentation of this impairment.	0 Severe dysphasia/aphasia affecting all modalities: auditory and reading comprehension inconsistent even at one key word. No meaningful expression.
1 Severe presentation of this impairment.	1 Severe dysphasia/aphasia: auditory and/or reading comprehension are consistent at one key word level. Occasionally understand and expresses limited amount.
2 Severe/moderate presentation.	2 Severe/moderate dysphasia/aphasia: auditory and/or reading comprehension consistent at a minimum of two or three key word level. Some limited verbal and/or written expression used appropriately and purposefully.
3 Moderate presentation.	3 Moderate dysphasia/aphasia: constant auditory and/or reading comprehension for simple sentences or structures. Inconsistent with complex commands and structures. Consistently reduced verbal and/or written language structure and vocabulary. May have a specific more severe difficulty in one modality.
4 Just below normal/mild impairment.	4 Mild dysphasia/aphasia: occasional difficulties present in auditory and/or reading comprehension and in verbal and/or written expression.
5 No impairment.	5 No dysphasia/aphasia.

The TOM, as adapted for different patient/client groups, was used in the study to assess the validity of the information gained over a period of time. It aimed to assess whether the TOM provides valid information on the changes effected during intervention. This was done by feeding back the data to the therapists and ascertaining whether the results obtained did reflect typical changes effected in their patients/clients, and whether the results could be used to inform therapists and to allow them to make inferences from the data. Face validity was established from this method.

The authors recognise that this TOM data sample was collected only over a short period of time on specific patient/client samples and therefore it was hard to assess change in long-term cases. The benchmark study (Enderby et al. 1999; John, 2001) allowed the authors to collect data over a longer period of time and to gain feedback from the therapists using the tool on whether the TOM captured significant clinical change. Typical changes were identified for different client groups, which allowed therapists to make inferences from the TOM data. The assessment of the validity of TOM has been made at face and content level in our own studies. Validity has also been tested in other studies such as that by Roulstone et al., who compared the TOM ratings on children's speech and language with the results from formal assessments and found positive correlations (Roulstone et al. 2004).

RELIABILITY

Reliability is an important feature of an outcome measure concerning the stability and consistency of a measure. Three reliability trials were carried out during the development of the TOM (1993, 1995, 1999). The aim was to establish the reliability of the TOM through undertaking three iterative studies. These results have been reported in the TOM Manuals (1997 and 1998) and in the benchmarking trial (Therapy Outcome Measures Benchmarking Study, 1998–1999 Enderby et al. 1999; John, 2002) and in other studies (Hammerton, 2004; Ryan, 2003).

These reliability trials indicated encouraging results, as assessed by the KAPPA and the inter-rater reliability coefficient (Streiner and Norman, 1989; Cohen, 1968; Maclure and Willett, 1987). The generalisability theory approach to assessing reliability was not used, as the TOM rating scale used ordinal data. Undertaking clinical reliability studies with patients/clients is difficult. There are concerns about exposing patients/clients and their relatives to a group of observers who independently assess and gauge the responses on a range of tasks. However, video and audio information, along with case notes, can be either inadequate or reveal information in such a way as to prime the judges. Many reliability studies have investigated the relationship between the scores of two independent judges assessing an individual patient/client. However, this does not give sufficient information to look at the range of agreement/disagreement in a broad range of observers who have different skills, backgrounds and philosophies.

In developing this tool, inter-rater reliability trials have been conducted and reported. The results of these iterative studies suggest that it is easier to obtain a high degree of reliability in the areas of impairment and disability, as these are areas regularly judged by therapists. The dimensions of impairment and activity can more easily be tested or observed while gaining accurate information in order to judge participation and well-being open to wider interpretation. The authors have found that judging participation and well-being from only case study information and video clip can result in variation in judgements because of paucity of information. Conversely, the authors found that where therapists have good information garnered from actual cases, a good level of intra- and inter-rater reliability was achieved (John, 1993).

As stated, the reliability of therapists using the TOM was tested using an iterative process. In the testing of the TOM as a benchmarking tool, therapists were recruited from 11 different NHS Services. In each service, the therapists were trained on the TOM in two 2½-hour sessions, asked to practice using the TOM on ten of their own patients/clients and then given a reliability check. The results were analysed using an inter-class correlation. These are shown in Tables 1-10 and 1-11. The therapists rated cases from case histories and viewing video clip. The therapists obtained good to almost perfect reliability on the TOM dimensions. Where lower reliability was obtained (Trial 6), an extra session was completed to resolve training issues through shared rating on the TOM. The reliability was then checked again, and reliability had increased (Trial 7).

On the dimensions of impairment, disability/activity and participation, more services had the highest level inter-rater reliability of "almost perfect", while the more subjective areas of handicap/participation and well-being demonstrated more variability in the ratings. In reflecting on these results, it is suggested that these dimensions might have benefited from more information in the test case histories to clarify points, particularly as the area of well-being is hard to capture in a "snap shot" where there was a loss of non-verbal clues that would have been experienced

Table 1-10. Reliability of 120 SLTs.

Trial Number	Site Number	Number of SLTs	ICC results for TOM dimensions					Client Group
			Impairment	Disability/ Activity	Social Participation	Well-being	Carer Well-being	
1	A and B	11	0.88	0.90	0.89	0.91	–	Adult
2	B	18	0.94	0.91	0.83	0.93	–	Child
3	C	7	0.90	0.90	0.90	0.90	–	Adult
4	C	15	0.90	0.87	0.81	0.77	0.79	Child
5	D	6	0.81	0.90	0.88	0.84	–	Adult
6	D	21	0.84	0.77	0.70	0.70	0.74	Child
7	E	4	0.61	0.78	0.73	0.40	–	Adult[a]
8	E	3	0.73	0.77	0.67	0.72	–	Adult[b]
9	E	9	0.84	0.91	0.91	0.89	0.77	Child
10	F	7	0.94	0.95	0.91	0.95	–	Adult
11	F	11	0.92	0.82	0.82	0.75	0.90	Child
12	G	3	0.86	0.88	0.79	0.83	–	Adult
13	G	6	0.85	0.85	0.72	0.72	0.87	Child

Notes: SLT = speech and language therapists.
[a] Adult team first reliability trial.
[b] Adult team second reliability trial.

Table 1-11. Inter-rater reliability of PT/OT/RN.

Trial Number	Site Number	Therapy Group	Number of Therapists	Coefficient of Reliability for					See Note Below
				Impairment	Disability/ Activity	Social Participation	Client Well-being	Carer Well-being	
1	A	PT	4	0.83	0.67	0.83	0.78	–	1
2	A	PT	2	0.83	0.98	0.90	0.93	–	2
3	A	PT	3	0.86	0.82	0.77	0.91	–	3
4	A	PT	2	0.96	1	1	0.95	–	4
5	A	PT	2	0.89	1	1	1	–	5
6	A	OT	3	0.74	0.92	0.77	0.80	0.87	6
7	B	OT	14	0.66	*0.52*	0.71	0.77	*0.58*	8[a]
8	B	OT	4	0.79	*0.47*	0.98	0.96	–	8[b]
9	B	OT	7	0.60	*0.51*	0.58	0.84	0.89	9[a]
10	B	OT	3	0.95	0.99	0.93	0.98	0.91	9[a]
11	C	PT	10	0.91	0.88	0.84	0.75	0.76	7/11
12	C	PT	7	0.29	0.42	0.54	0.45	0.54	11[a]
13	C	PT	9	0.67	0.86	0.69	0.60	0.84	11[b]
14	C	PT/OT	4	0.99	0.96	0.98	0.99	1	12
15	C	PT	4	0.81	0.84	0.61	0.81	*0.57*	7
16	C	PT	11	0.83	0.82	0.82	0.85	0.86	13
17	D	OT	4	0.80	0.68	0.66	0.87	0.88	10
18	D	PT	8	0.88	0.91	0.91	0.90	0.88	10
19	E	OT	6	0.75	0.68	*0.43*	0.74	0.77	2/13[a]
20	E	OT	11	0.85	0.89	0.86	0.87	–	2/13[b]
21	E	OT	8	0.62	0.67	0.75	0.87	0.74	11[a]
22	E	OT	10	0.85	0.94	0.88	0.98	0.97	11[b]
23	E	OT	9	0.85	0.90	0.93	0.91	–	8/14

Table 1-11. *(continued)*

Trial Number	Site Number	Therapy Group	Number of Therapists	Coefficient of Reliability for					See Note Below
				Impairment	Disability/ Activity	Social Participation	Client Well-being	Carer Well-being	
24	G	PT	5	0.67	0.87	0.76	0.77	0.50	10
25	G	PT	4	0.69	0.87	0.79	0.86	–	11
26	H	OT/RN	4	0.83	0.71	0.73	0.79	0.82	8
27	I	OT	6	0.42	0.67	0.53	0.82	0.60	12
28	I	PT	8	0.73	0.69	0.67	0.85	0.61	12

Notes:
1. Therapists dealing with spinal problems.
2. Therapists dealing with neurology.
3. Therapists dealing with fractures.
4. Therapists dealing with amputees.
5. Therapists dealing with rheumatoid arthritis.
6. Therapists dealing with adults.
7. Therapists dealing with children.
8. Rehabilitation therapist.
9. Mental health therapist.
10. Community paediatric team.
11. Community team.
12. Learning and disabilities team.
13. Outpatients /clients team.
14. Mixed team.

PT = physiotherapists; OT = occupational therapists; RN = rehabilitation nursing.
[a] First trial.
[b] Second trial.

by the therapists in the natural setting. In order to make a judgement, the therapists may have to observe the style of response to judge the degree of emotional well-being for themselves and may need different information to make a decision on rating. In the TOM pilot studies (see Chapter 4 p. 76, John, 1993), reliability was higher on these subjective areas when therapists were rating real cases that were known to the therapists.

In the team rating of the adult client videotapes and case histories, the therapists were not asked to rate the carer well-being, as many of the case studies did not have a carer profile on which to base decisions. The SLTs treating adults generally had very good reliability on all dimensions of the TOM. In Service E the adult team had lower levels of reliability on TOM because one SLT consistently rated cases lower than the others. This demonstrated a severity bias and lowered the overall levels of reliability for that team. The results of the reliability check were fed back to the team and the reasons for rating lower were explored through discussion and further training on the TOM. This took the form of team discussion of rating of cases and joint rating, in order to explore differences. A repeat of the reliability check resulted in higher inter-rater reliability for the team (Trial 7).

In the PT/OT/RN reliability trial, each group rated 10 cases from their own caseload using composite case histories. It was not possible to use video clips in this study because few of the services had those facilities. In the reliability study, we found more variation in rating within some teams than others. The teams that treated similar cases had very good reliability. This can be attributed to the fact that they shared a common knowledge of the real cases. However, in the services where therapists did not know each other's cases and had to rely on less familiar information, the reliability was more variable. Also, reliability was best in those services where the therapists had completed the full training and had used the TOM to rate their own cases for a practice period. We discovered that some of the participating therapists had not completed this requirement prior to taking part in the reliability check. Training played an important part in achieving reliability. Where a service had a low level of reliability, further training improved the level of inter-rater reliability achieved. Table 1-11 shows this pattern for Trials 1 and 2.

Bias on the part of the rater/observer is a problem encountered when using a subjective measure, and a number of biases have been described in the literature (Bailey, 1997; Everitt, 1994; Streiner and Norman, 1989; Beutler and Hamblin, 1986; Newble et al. 1980; Saal et al. 1980). These can be summarised as including:

- ***Halo***: an inability to discriminate on a scale the distinct features or behaviours of the individual rated.
- ***Leniency or severity***: constantly giving a lower or a higher rating than ratee's ability.
- ***Range restriction***: use of only part of the scale when rating using a limited range in the low, mid or high points. Also referred to as "Central Tendency" or "End Aversion".

The presence of observer bias, once identified, can be ameliorated either through further training, where possible, or where this is not feasible it may be necessary to exclude those observers whose bias cannot be controlled (Newble et al. 1980). We found that further training for some therapists reduced bias and increased reliability.

BENCHMARKING

Principle and Background

The concepts of benchmarking and outcomes in healthcare are inextricably linked to that of "quality", which has increasingly been a focus for those charged with the provision of care. Evaluation of quality requires a decision on what to measure, from whose perspective, what form of measurement to use, who should undertake the measurement, how to analyse data and, finally, how the information gained will be disseminated and acted upon. The information on quality needs to be put into context if correct interpretation is to be made. One means of achieving this is through the use of appropriate comparisons and an awareness of the nature of the variations observed. For example, there may be comparisons against established objectives, standards and guidelines or against patient/client needs and expectations; comparisons can then be performed within a health service, or can be used to compare results with a similar service or services. Benchmarking is one approach in making useful comparisons to inform change (MacDonald and Tanner, 1998) by identifying the process steps and outcomes, thus establishing a baseline for current practice, and comparing that with other similar services to identify aspects of best practice (Bullivant, 1996; Bullivant and Roberts, 1997; Codling, 1996). Variations can be investigated in order to ascertain the reasons for differences in organisations, processes and outcomes of care. Such information, combined with clinical expertise, can support clinical decision-making, and changes can be effected to improve the quality of care (Mulley, 1999).

MacDonald and Tanner (1998) described benchmarking as a cycle to "Plan, Collect, Analyse and Adapt", where each step can be defined as appropriate to meet particular needs. Table 1-12 illustrates a model developed by MacDonald and Tanner (1998) of the benchmarking steps for executing the benchmarking of a service.

Another approach developed by the National Health Service Benchmarking Reference Centre (BRC) suggest a 12-stage process (Bullivant and Roberts, 1997), which conforms to MacDonald and Tanner's four-point process detailed in Table 1-12.

1. Identify the benchmark topic (ensuring relevance and interest).
2. Define the goals, conducting an initial process mapping exercise on the project's stages (e.g. considering relevant stakeholders).
3. Identify what information and indicators are needed.
4. Identify project workers (ensuring that senior management is committed).
5. Collect the information and identify and recruit appropriate benchmark partners.
6. Analyse the data, comparing data and shortfalls in performance.

Table 1-12. A benchmarking process model from MacDonald and Tanner (1998).

Step	Activity	Process
Step 1	Plan the study	Form a benchmarking team. Establish the process, outcome to be benchmarked. Document the current process, expected outcomes. Define the topic areas for data collection. Identify potential benchmarking partners.
Step 2	Collect the data	Plan data-collection methods. Conduct a primary investigation. Prepare for site visits. Conduct site visits. Write site visit report.
Step 3	Analyse the data	Normalise performance data. Construct a comparison matrix. Identify best practices. Isolate process enablers.
Step 4	Adapt	Communicate findings and gain a commitment to change. Set goals to close the gaps. Adapt enablers. Develop an implementation plan and implement it. Monitor and report progress.

7. Identify differences and visit “beacon” service providers to exchange information and identify practices for the Action Plan.
8. Set performance targets for service, together with goals for change.
9. Communicate findings and disseminate information within service; establish a timescale for change.
10. Establish a team capable of managing the change.
11. Implement changes.
12. Review progress and benchmark.

TOM Benchmarking

The TOM has been used as a benchmarking tool to benchmark outcomes of care (Enderby and John, 1999; Enderby et al. 2000; John, 2002; John et al. 2001, 2005a, 2005b). Therapists from different services were trained on the TOM, established their reliability on the measure and collected data on consecutive cases over an 18-month period. The TOM data was analysed on the TOM data analysis programme (Petheram at Speech and Language Therapy Research Unit, Frenchay Hospital, Bristol) and this provided the average rating on each dimension for all cases. This aggregated rating was the "benchmark" for all cases. The data for individual sites had their own benchmark which could be compared with the overall benchmark for all cases and against other sites. Foe example, therapists were able to look at their own outcome results for individual client groups, as well as compare these outcomes with that of therapists in the same service to complete internal benchmarking. Also, they could compare their outcome results with that of other services and with the aggregated data for a specific client group (external benchmarking). The data generated by the TOM was able to show typical start ratings, change and final ratings, contacts, duration of treatment and reason for discharge. Therapists from each service were able to add meaning to the data to aid the interpretation of the meaning of the data. Examples of the TOM benchmarking studies in speech and language therapy, physiotherapy and occupational therapy are now summarised to illustrate the information that can be yielded by this approach. The results are shown in the following text by way of illustration.

Benchmarking Results

Speech and Language Therapy

The TOM benchmarking study had eight SLT services participating. There were 4856 cases entered into the TOM benchmarking study from the eight Service sites. This number does not represent all the cases seen by SLTs within a Service, but represents those cases that had either completed their treatment or an episode of care. Therefore, those cases that were assessed but did not receive an intervention, or with only one rating, are not represented. The 4856 cases entered into the study had an entry code of "A" for admission rating, or "I" for intermediate rating.

The data analysed using the Statistical Package for Social Sciences (SPSS Version 10) frequency analysis of the cases entered by "Aetiology" code found that the largest number of cases was in the category of "nothing abnormal detected", which represented those cases with no evident aetiological condition. Of those cases that did have a known aetiological condition, "learning difficulty" formed the largest group (514 cases) followed by "acquired neurological" (487 cases). The cases entering the study were coded across 21 different disorder codes. Of the disorder codes, the disorders of "developmental language impairment" (1576 cases) and "developmental phonological impairment" (1190 cases), accounted for 56% of the cases with a primary disorder.

The data could be selected for analysis according to the question being asked, such as the following:

1. Do clients have an equal opportunity of accessing speech and language therapy services according to their abilities and regardless of where they are treated?
2. Does the application of speech and language therapy produce similar changes in clients' abilities and/or disabilities regardless of where the treatment is provided?
3. Do clients have similar profiles of abilities and/or disabilities on discharge irrespective of where they are treated?

In this illustration, the data from cases with a dysphasia will be used to show how data can be benchmarked to provide outcome profiles for comparison at an internal or external level. The statistical results are shown in Table 1-13.

There were 197 cases admitted to treatment with dysphasia. The following data analysis results show how data can be analysed at different levels.

Aetiology

The prominent aetiology associated with dysphasia was an acquired neurological condition arising from a cerebral vascular accident. There was no significant difference between Service in the range of aetiologies associated with dysphasia.

Age

Of the 197 cases admitted to treatment, the mean age was 67.7 years and the median age on admission was 71.4 years. There was a very significant difference across the Services in the age of the cases on entry to treatment and on exit from treatment. However, there was no significant difference in the age and TOM start rating.

Start Ratings

The median start rating of patients/clients with dysphasia on all the TOM dimensions was 3 (indicating moderate difficulties). The trend was for those cases that entered treatment with a more severe start rating on impairment to have more contacts, and to be in treatment longer, than those cases with milder difficulties. There was no significant difference in start ratings across the seven Services. On the face of it, therefore, it appears that the cases had equal access to treatment.

Final Ratings

The median final rating was 3.5 on impairment and 4 for the other dimensions. There was a similarity in the final ratings on impairment, disability/activity, participation

Table 1-13. Summary of the statistical analysis of TOM data for dysphasia.

Variable	TOM Dimension	All Cases Statistic, Mean, Median, and %	Statistic across Services
Age median 197 cases		mean 67.7 years median 71.4 years	Significant**
Age/start rating 197 cases	Impairment Activity Participation Well-being Carer well-being	Not significant Not significant Not significant Not significant Not significant	
Start rating 197 cases	Impairment Activity Participation Well-being Carer well-being	3 3 3 3 3	Not significant Not significant Not significant Not significant Not significant
Final rating 142 cases	Impairment Activity Participation Well-being Carer well-being	3.5 4 4 4 4	Not significant Not significant Not significant Significant** Not significant
Direction of change showing the percentage of cases making a positive change	Impairment Activity Participation Well-being Carer well-being	70% 70% 74% 77% 75%	Significant* Significant* Not significant Not significant Not significant
Contacts	–	Mean 15.3 Median 8	Significant***
Duration	–	Mean 6.2 months Median 3.6 months	Significant***
Reason for discharge	'Treatment Complete'	70%	Significant***
Reason for discharge and final rating	Impairment Activity Participation Well-being Carer well-being	Significant*** Significant*** Significant*** Significant*** Not significant	

* $p < 0.05$; ** $p < 0.01$; *** $p < 0.001$.

and carer well-being. Overall, the cases with dysphasia did not show a significant difference in final ratings across the Services, which demonstrated similar exit points from treatment on the TOM rating scale. The exception was in the dimension of well-being, which demonstrated a highly significant difference across the Services. For example, variation was noted in one Service (2) which had a median final rating higher than the benchmark, while another Service had the widest range of final ratings, and a different Service had a lower final rating.

Contacts and Duration of Treatment

The results from the TOM benchmarking study indicated that some of the Services offered consistently fewer contacts, and had a shorter duration of treatment, than cases receiving treatment in the other Services. Furthermore, there was considerable variation within the individual Services in what was provided.

On the associated variables of contacts and duration of treatment, there was a highly significant difference across the Services in both the number of contacts provided and in the duration of treatment. For those cases that completed treatment, the median number of contacts was 8, with a duration of 3.6 months. On contacts, there was a variation in the number of SLT contacts received by cases in the different Services. For example, three Services had a higher number of contacts than the benchmark, while five Services had fewer contacts than the benchmark. Generally, the trend was for cases that entered treatment with a more severe start rating on impairment to receive more contacts than those cases that had a high start rating.

On duration of treatment, there was a highly significant difference between the Services, with marked variation also in the duration of treatment offered. The trend was for cases that entered treatment with a more severe start rating to be in treatment for longer than those with a milder impairment. That said, there was marked variation in the number of contacts and the duration of treatment offered by an individual Service to cases with dysphasia. Cases with the same level of impairment entering treatment within different Services received different levels of input in terms of contacts and duration. Thus, in practice, the severity of impairment was not an indication of the intensity of treatment that the cases received.

Reasons for Discharge from Care

Those cases that completed their program of treatment with the SLT had a better outcome, with a higher final rating, than cases which were, for different reasons, discharged. There was a highly significant difference across the Services on the reason for discharge from treatment, with some Services keeping cases on their caseload after treatment was completed, or discharging a case because it was unlikely that the individual would have reached his/her potential. The analysis found that there was a highly significant difference between the reason for discharge from treatment and the final ratings. On discharge from treatment, 70% of all cases that completed their full treatment programme were discharged at a higher rating point on the TOM than those cases that were discharged for other reasons. Interestingly, there was a highly significant difference across the Services in the reason that cases were discharged from treatment, and there was a highly significant difference between the reason for discharge and final ratings on the TOM: dimension impairment, disability/activity, participation and a very significant difference on well-being. Generally, those cases that completed their treatment with their SLT had the best outcome on the TOM dimensions.

Number of Cases Changing Direction

There was a significant difference across the Services in the number of cases making a change in direction on the dimensions of impairment and disability/activity. For example, there was variation on the number of cases sustaining their rating, so that on impairment, two Services were higher than the benchmark for "All Cases", and on disability/activity, three Services were higher than the benchmark for "All Cases". Also, one Service had more cases sustaining their rating as a percentage of the cases seen, as compared with the other Services. The majority of cases made a positive change on the TOM. On the number of cases changing direction on the TOM, 70% of cases made a positive change on impairment, 70% on disability/activity, 74% on participation, 77% on well-being and 75% on carer well-being. It is interesting to note that the dimensions of participation, well-being and carer well-being showed the greatest number of cases changing positively (John, 2001).

Table 1-13 shows a summary of the statistical analysis of the cases treated for dysphasia in eight separate SLT services.

Occupational Therapy

In the results of a benchmarking study, nine different occupational therapy services also looked at the entry, change and exit ratings on the TOM. The data set available for benchmark analysis was 1711 patients/clients treated from admission to discharge by OT with the study period. In the patients/client group "acquired neurological disease" there were 288 patients/clients in which there were 160 Cerebral Vascular Accident (CVA) cases, 22 head injury cases, 4 Guillan Barre patients/clients and 102 other "acquired neurological" conditions. It was found that "multi-factorial" was the most common reason for OT involvement, accounting for over half the patients/clients. The term "multi-factorial" was used when the patient/client had three or more causes to limit activity. A focus of interest to both therapists and managers will be how much average change has been achieved during the same time period of occupational therapy. The improvement of patients/clients was recorded on the scale – deteriorate, no change, one-unit, two-unit and three-unit improvement on the TOM measurement. It should be noted that for a patient/client scoring, say, 3 on the TOM handicap scale on admission, the maximum improvement is two points up to the ceiling of 5 on any TOM rating.

Table 1-14 shows the number of cases changing on each point of the rating scale on every TOM dimension for cases with an acquired neurological disease treated by OT.

Table 1-14. Improvement benchmarks in TOM: acquired neurological condition.

	% of Patients/Clients whom, by Discharge:						
Level of TOM at Admission	May Deteriorate	Show No Change	Improve by One Unit	Improve by Two Units	Improve by Three Units	Improve by Four Units	Improve by Five Units
Impairment							
0		56	11	11	11	11	0
1	3	50	15	24	8	0	
2	1	42	33	24	0		
3	4	41	45	11			
4	3	82	16				
5	0	100					
Activity							
0		44	31	13	0	6	6
1	3	17	32	29	16	2	
2	3	22	36	32	8		
3	5	25	55	15			
4	2	69	29				
5	0	100					

Table 1-14. (*continued*)

	% of Patients/Clients whom, by Discharge:						
Level of TOM at Admission	May Deteriorate	Show No Change	Improve by One Unit	Improve by Two Units	Improve by Three Units	Improve by Four Units	Improve by Five Units
Participation							
0		17	67	17	0	0	0
1	2	26	29	18	20	6	
2	3	30	28	35	5		
3	3	43	43	12			
4	6	67	27				
5	0	100					
Well-being							
0		33	33	0	11	11	11
1	0	14	32	0	43	11	
2	8	17	27	43	5		
3	0	42	49	9			
4	9	52	39				
5	10	90					

The amount of change made varies but typically cases change by one or two units from the point they are rated on entry to treatment. The general pattern that is observed overall dimensions is that the chances of improvement are clearly related to the level of admission score. For this group, deterioration at the time of treatment is a rare event, occurring in an average of 5% or less patients/clients. Treatment was associated with positive improvement, and while more than half of the patients/clients did not show improvement in all domains following treatment, a significant number did. The OT working with individuals with an acquired neurological deficit had as one of their primary goals the improvement of activity and performance while promoting a reduction in impairment. It is interesting that the overall benchmark showed that, while only over one-half of the patients/clients showed improvement in the area of impairment, more than three-quarters of the patients/clients improved in the area of activity. Any individual Service now has the capacity to compare their performance against these benchmarks. As an example, Service F generated the data shown in Table 1-15.

Table 1-15. Improvement in TOM for patients/clients with "acquired neurological disease" treated in Service F.

% of Patients/Clients whom, by Discharge:							
Level of TOM at Admission	May Deteriorate	Show No Change	Improve by One Unit	Improve by Two Units	Improve by Three Units	Improve by Four Units	Improve by Five Units
Impairment							
0		100 ↑	0 ↓	0 ↓	0 ↓	0 ↓	0
1	13 ↑	62 ↑	25 ↑	0 ↓	0 ↓	0	
2	0	50 ↑	25 ↓	25	0		
3	0	52 ↑	36 ↓	12			
4	8 ↑	88 ↑	4 ↓				
5	0	100					
Disability							
0		25 ↓	38 ↑	12	0	12 ↑	12 ↑
1	0	19	32	22 ↓	24 ↑	0	
2	4	14 ↓	25 ↓	36	21 ↑		
3	7	20 ↓	40 ↓	33 ↑			
4	0	86 ↑	14 ↓				
5							

Table 1-15. *(continued)*

	% of Patients/Clients whom, by Discharge:						
Level of TOM at Admission	May Deteriorate	Show No Change	Improve by One Unit	Improve by Two Units	Improve by Three Units	Improve by Four Units	Improve by Five Units
Handicap							
0		0 ↓	50 ↓	50 ↑	0	0	0
1	0	21 ↓	35 ↑	14	21	10	
2	4	18 ↓	27	47 ↑	4		
3	0	37 ↓	42	21 ↑			
4	17 ↑	50 ↓	33 ↑				
5	0	100					
Well-being							
0		0 ↓	100 ↑	0	0 ↓	0 ↓	0 ↓
1	0	22 ↑	33	0	33 ↓	0 ↓	
2	9	5 ↓	36 ↑	41	9		
3	0	40	40 ↓	20 ↑			
4	9	41 ↓	50 ↑				
5	0 ↓	100 ↑					

In considering the performance of this Service, it would first be necessary to identify all the cells in Table 1-15 that differ by more than (say) 5% from the benchmark equivalent data (i.e. Table 1-15). The difference may indeed be a figure above the equivalent benchmark value (marked with ↑) or a figure below the benchmark value (marked with ↓). Finally it is necessary to look at the overall pattern of arrows. A Service that is doing better than the benchmark will have ↓ in the two columns of "May deteriorate" and "Show no change", and ↑ as far to the right as possible in the five "Improve" columns. A Service that is performing below the benchmark will have ↑ in the first two columns and ↓ in the other columns (Enderby et al. 2003).

Service F must, therefore, be considered to be:

under-performing on areas of activity likely to improve impairment;
performing marginally better than the benchmark on disability/activity;
performing marginally better than the benchmark on handicap/participation; or
performing close to the benchmark in respect of patient/client well-being.

Physiotherapy

As shown in the previously presented data samples, the TOM data can be aggregated for different benchmarking purposes. In addition to the examples of analysis presented for SLT and OT, further analysis can be completed for specific conditions. Data is presented here for cases that received physiotherapy for musculoskeletal conditions (Enderby et al. 2000). Table 1-16 shows the data analysis for 1207 cases with a musculoskeletal condition who completed treatment from five physiotherapy services. Note that very few carers were rated; typically the carers who were rated on well-being were carers of children and individuals who were 70-plus years of age.

It can be observed that Service D and E had cases of similar ages but had different patterns of service delivery as seen in the hours, duration and number of contacts provided during intervention. Tables 1-17 to 1-21 show the start, change and finish ratings and percentage change for each TOM dimension by Service and overall

Table 1-16. PT – musculoskeletal numbers, age, hours, duration and contacts.

PT – Musculoskeletal Service and Benchmark	No. of Cases Completing Treatment	No. of Carers	Mean Age in Years	Hours	Duration in Months	Contacts
Service A	7	7	3.6	17	8.5	23.4
Service B	43	10	72.5	3.7	2.9	6.9
Service C	1132	14	45.2	2.8	1.5	5.7
Service D	44	8	53.5	3.0	1.4	5.8
Service E	8	5	54	3.8	5.2	3.9
Total cases and benchmark	1207	30	46.5	2.9	1.5	5.7

Table 1-17. PT – musculoskeletal impairment.

PT – Musculoskeletal Complete	Impairment Start	Impairment Finish	Impairment Change	Impairment % Change
Service A	2.1	3.4	1.2	22.8
Service B	2.5	3.3	0.7	12.5
Service C	3.2	4.3	1.1	15.1
Service D	2.8	4.2	1.4	19.9
Service E	2.4	2.6	0.2	3.9
Benchmark	3.1	4.2	1.1	15.2

Table 1-18. PT – musculoskeletal disability/activity.

PT – Musculoskeletal Complete	Disability/ Activity Start	Disability/ Activity Finish	Disability/ Activity Change	Disability/ Activity % Change
Service A	2.3	3.7	1.4	26.9
Service B	3	3.5	0.5	8.7
Service C	3.9	4.6	0.7	8.8
Service D	4	4.3	0.4	4.8
Service E	2.8	2.9	0.1	2.5
Benchmark	3.8	4.5	0.7	8.7

benchmark. Cases in Service E made the least change on three of the TOM dimensions: i.e. impairment, disability/activity, participation, and provided the fewest number of contacts.

It is of interest that, when a comparison was made between the different services within Services, it was observed that in two instances the OT service provided intervention to an older age group than the PT service (Table 1-22) and the occupational therapy intervention provided more contacts than the average PT intervention.

Table 1-19. PT – musculoskeletal participation.

PT – Musculoskeletal Complete	Participation Start	Participation Finish	Participation Change	Participation % Change
Service A	4.1	4.4	0.2	2.7
Service B	3.3	3.6	0.3	3.2
Service C	3.9	4.5	0.7	8.4
Service D	3.9	4.3	0.4	5.6
Service E	2.6	2.7	0.1	1.1
Benchmark	3.9	4.5	0.6	8.1

Table 1-20. PT – musculoskeletal patient/client well-being.

PT – Musculoskeletal Complete	Patient/Client Well-being Start	Patient/Client Well-being Finish	Patient/Client Well-being Change	Patient/Client Well-being % Change
Service A	4.2	4.6	0.4	4.3
Service B	3.6	4	0.4	5.1
Service C	4.4	4.8	0.4	5.4
Service D	4.7	4.9	0.2	2.3
Service E	3.9	4.1	0.2	2.2
Benchmark	4.3	4.7	0.4	5.2

Conclusion

The TOM benchmarking study aimed to use routinely collected outcome data to provide benchmark profiles that could inform therapists. The analysis of TOM data to answer specific questions has highlighted both similarities and differences between Services. The benchmarking process enabled the participating therapists to compare their data with that of the overall benchmark for all cases (internal benchmarking) and then to compare this with other Services to identify best performance (external benchmarking). In any Service, the aim would be to complete the benchmarking

Table 1-21. PT – musculoskeletal carer well-being.

PT – Musculoskeletal Complete	Carer Well-being Start	Carer Well-being Finish	Carer Well-being Change	Carer Well-being % Change
Service A	3.3	4.1	0.8	11.3
Service B	4	4.3	0.3	3.1
Service C	4	4.6	0.6	8.4
Service D	4.5	4.6	0.1	1.4
Service E	4.7	4.9	0.2	2
Benchmark	4.1	4.5	0.5	6

Table 1-22. OT and PT musculoskeletal cases; age and contacts.

Services OT	OT Age in Years	OT Contacts	PT Age in Years	PT Contacts
Service B	71.2	14.1	72.5	6.9
Service C	70	7.8	45.2	5.8
Service D	74.5	16.4	53.5	3.9
Benchmark for all services	61.2	28.2	46.5	5.7

process by linking the process to outcomes and to investigate how information could be used to effect change to improve Services and the outcomes of that Service. Staff and patient/client characteristics are important details to record along with process and outcome data.

The benchmarking process is cyclical and should be repeated in order to identify whether any changes in service have resulted in better outcomes. It is proposed that benchmarking has the potential to inform therapists on aspects of their practice and performance by using tools employed in routine clinical practice. The use of benchmark data, combined with meaning, can thereby provide information that can help therapists to build a picture of performance and engender change for quality improvement.

REFERENCES

Anderson, J., Sullivan, F., and Usherwood, T. (1990) The medical outcomes study instrument (MOST): Use of a new health status measure in Britain. *Family Practice*, 7, 205–218.

Andrews, F. and Crandall, R. (1976) The validity of measures of self-reported well-being. *Social Indicators Research*, 6, 1–19.

Austin, C. and Clark, C. R. (1993) Measures of outcome: From whom? *British Journal of Occupational Therapy*, 56, 21–24.

Bailey, D. M. (1997) *Research for the Health Professional: A Practical Guide*. Philadelphia, PA, F.A. Davis Company.

Behi, R. and Nolan, M. (1995) Reliability: consistency and accuracy in measurement. *British Journal of Nursing*, 4, 472–533.

Beutler, L. E. and Hamblin, D. L. (1986) Individualised outcome measures of internal change: Methodological considerations. *Journal of Consulting and Clinical Psychology*, 54, 48–53.

Blomert, L. (1990) What functional assessment can contribute to setting goals for aphasia therapy. *Aphasiology*, 4, 307–320.

Bryman, A. (1988) *Quantity and Quality in Social Research*. London, UNWIN Hyman.

Buetow, S. A. and Roland, M. (1999) Clinical governance: Bridging the gap between managerial and clinical approaches to quality of care. *Quality in Health Care*, 8, 184–190.

Bullivant, J. (1996) Benchmarking in the UK NHS. *International Journal of Health Care Quality Assurance* 9, 9–14.

Bullivant, J. and Roberts, A. (1997) Service benchmarking: to choose to improve. Health service manager. *Special Report, 14*, Kingston upon Thames, Croner Publications, 1–16.

Codling, S. (1996) *Best Practice Benchmarking: An International Perspective*. Aldershot, Gower.

Cohen, J. (1968) Weighted kappa: Nominal scale agreement with provision for scaled disagreement or partial credit. *Psychological Bulletin*, 70, 213–220.

Cowley, A. J., Fullwood, L. J., Muller, A. F., Stainer, K., Skene, A. M., and Hampton, J. R. (1991) Exercise capability in heart failure: Is cardiac output important after all. *Lancet*, 33, 771–773.

Department of Health. (1989) *Working for Patient/Clients. (Cm. 555)*. London, H.M.S.O.

Department of Health. (1999) *Clinical Governance: Quality in the New NHS*. London. H.M.S.O.

Department of Health. (1999a) *Governance in the New NHS*. London. H.M.S.O.

Department of Health. (1999b) *Governance in the New NHS: Annex A (123)*. London, H.M.S.O.

Donaldson, S., Wagner, C., and Gresham, G. (1973) A unified ADL evaluation form, *Archives Physical Medicine Rehabilitation*, 54(4), 175–179.

Donovan, J. L., Frankel, S. J., and Eyles, J. D. (1993) Assessing the need for health status measures. *Journal of Epidemiology and Community Health* 47, 158–162.

Ebrahim, S., Nouri, F., and Barer, D. (1985) Measuring disability after a stroke, *Journal of Epidemiology and Community Health*, 39, 86–89.

Enderby, P. (1981) *Frenchay Dysarthria Assessment Frenchay Dysarthria Assessment*, San Diego, USA College Hill Press.

Enderby, P. (1992) Outcome measures in speech therapy: Impairment, disability, handicap, and distress. *Health Trends*, 24, 61–64.

Enderby, P. (1999) *For richer for poorer: outcome measurement in speech and language therapy*. Advances in speech language pathology volume 1 number one pp. 63–65.

Enderby, P., Hughes, A., John, A., and Petheram, B. (2003) Using benchmark data for assessing performance in occupational therapy. *Clinical Governance: An International Journal*, 8(4), 290–295.

Enderby, P. and John, A. (1997) *Therapy Outcome Measures: Speech-Language Pathology*. San Diego: London, Singular Publishing Group.

Enderby, P. and John, A. (1999) Therapy outcome measures in speech and language therapy: Comparing performance between different providers. *International Journal of Language and Communication Disorders*, 34, 417–429.

Enderby, P., John, A., Hughes, A., and Petheram, B. (2000) Benchmarking in rehabilitation: comparing physiotherapy services. *British Journal of Clinical Governance*, 5(2), 86–92.

Enderby, P., John, A., and Petheram, B. (1998) *Therapy Outcome Measures: Physiotherapy, Occupational Therapy, Rehabilitation Nursing*. San Diego: London, Singular Publishing Group.

Enderby, P., John, A., and Petheram, B. (1998–1999) *Therapy Outcome Measures Benchmarking Study*, Institute of General Practice and Primary Care, SCHARR, University of Sheffield.

Enderby, P., John, A., Sloan, M., and Petheram, B. (1995) *Outcome Measures in Speech and language Therapy*. Bristol, Speech and Language Therapy Research Unit.

Enderby, P., John, A., Hughes, A., and Petheram, B. (1999) *Therapy Outcome Measures Benchmarking Report*. University of Sheffield.

Enderby, P. and Kew, E. (1995) *Outcome measurements in physiotherapy using the World Health Organisation's classification of impairment, disability and handicap: a pilot study*. Physiotherapy. Volume 81 number four pp. 177–183.

Everitt, B. S. (1994) Statistical methods for medical investigations. *Measurement in Medicine*. New York, John Wiley & Sons.

Frattali, C. (1991) Professional practices perspective. *American Speech & Hearing Association*, 33, 12.

Fugl-Meyer, A. R., Branholm, I. B., and Fugl-Meyer, K. S. (1991) Happiness and domain specific life satisfaction in adult Northern Swedes. *Clinical Rehabilitation*, 5, 25–33.

Gamiats, T. G., Palinkas, L. A., and Kaplan, R. (1992) Comparison of quality of wellbeing scale and functional status index in patient/clients with atrial fibrillation. *Medical Care* 30, 958–964.

Goldberg, D. (1992) *General Health Questionnaire (GHQ-12)*. Windsor, UK: NFER-Nelson.

Guildford, J. P. (1954) *Psychometric Methods*. New York: McGraw-Hill.

Haley, S. M., Coster, W. L., and Ludlow, L. H. (1991) Paediatric functional outcome measures. *Physical Medicine and Rehabilitation Clinics of North America*, 2, 89–723.

Hammersley, M. (1987) Some notes on the terms "validity" and "reliability". *British Educational Research Journal*, 13, 73–81.

Hammerton, J. (2004) *An Investigation into the Influence of Age on Recovery from Stroke with Community Rehabilitation*. PhD Thesis, University of Sheffield.

Harewood, R., Jitapunkul, S., Dickinson, E., and Ebrahim, S. (1994) Measuring handicap: Motives, methods, and a model. *Quality in Health Care*, 3, 53–57.

Health Care Advisory Board. (1994) Quality measures: Next generation of outcome tracking. *The Advisory Board*, 2(25), 32.

Hopkins, A. Medical audit: A second report. (1993) *Journal of Royal College of Physicians London*, 27(2), 131–2.

Hunt, S., McEven, J. (1980) The development of a subjective health indicator. *Social Health Illness*, 2, 231–246.

John, A. (1993) *An Outcome Measure for Language Impaired Children Under Six Years: A Study of Reliability and Validity*. MSc. Thesis, City University.

John, A. (2002) *Therapy Outcome Measures for Benchmarking in Speech and Language Therapy*. Ph.D. Thesis, University of Sheffield.

John, A. and Enderby, P. (2000) Reliability of speech and language therapists using therapy outcome measures. *International Journal of Language and Communication Disorders*, 35, 287–302.

John, A., Enderby, P., and Hughes, A. (2005a) Benchmarking outcomes in dysphasia using the therapy outcome measure. *Aphasiology*, 19(2), 165–178.

John, A., Enderby, P., and Hughes, A. (2005b) Comparing outcomes of voice therapy: A benchmarking study using the therapy outcome measure. *Journal of Voice*, 19(1), 114–123.

John, A., Enderby, P., Hughes, A., and Petheram. B. (2001) Benchmarking can facilitate the sharing of information on outcomes of care. *International Journal of Language and Communication Disorders*, 36 Suppl. 385–390.

Long, A. (1996) The user perspective in outcome measure: An overview of the issues. *Outcomes Briefings* 8, 4–8.

MacDonald, J. and Tanner, S. (1998) *Understanding Benchmarking*. London, Hodder & Stoughton.

Maclure, M. and Willett, W. C. (1987) Misinterpretation and misuse of the Kappa statistic. *American Journal of Epidemiology*, 126, 161–169.

McCrae, R. R. and Costa, P. T. (1986) Personality, coping and coping effectiveness in an adult sample. *Journal of Personality*, 2, 285–405.

McKenna, S. P., Hunt, S. M., and Tennant, A. (1993) The development of a patient/client completed index of distress from the nottingham health profile: A new measure for use in cost utility studies. *British Journal of Medical Economics*, 6, 13–24.

Meenan, R., Gertman, P., and Mason, J. (1980) Measuring health status in arthritis. *Arthritis and Rheumatism*, 23(2), 146–152.

Melzack, R. Ed. (1983) *Pain Measurement in Assessment*. New York, Raven Press.

Mulley, A. G. (1999) Learning from differences within the NHS. *British Medical Journal*, 319, 528–530.

Newble, D. I., Hoare, J., and Sheldrake, P. F. (1980) The selection and training of examiners for clinical examinations. *Medical Education*, 4, 345–349.

Nolan, M. and Behi, R. (1995) Alternative approaches to establishing reliability and validity. *British Journal of Nursing*, 4, 587–590.

Øvretveit, J. (1992) *Health Service Quality*. Oxford, Blackwell Scientific Press.

Øvretveit, J. (1998) *Evaluating Health Interventions.* Buckingham: Philadelphia, PA, Open University Press.

Paterson, C. (1996) Measuring outcomes in primary care: a patient/client generated measure. MYMOP compared with SF36 health survey. *British Medical Journal*, 312, 106–1020.

Patrick, D., Dareby, S., Green, S., Horton, G., Locker, D., and Wiggins, R. (1981) Screening for disability in the inner city. *Journal of Epidemiology and Community Health*, 35, 65–70.

Reisenberg, D. and Glass, R. (1989) The medical outcomes study. *JAMA*, 262(7), 943.

Rosser, R. M. (1976) Recent studies using a global approach to measuring illness. *Medical Care*, 14, (Suppl 5), 138–147.

Roulstone, S., John, A., Hughes, A., and Enderby, P. (2004) Assessing the construct validity of the therapy outcome measure for pre-school children with delayed speech and language. *Advances in Speech-Language Pathology*, 6(4), 230–236.

Ryan, A. (2003) *An Evaluation of Intensity of Community Based Multidisciplinary Therapy Following Stroke or Hip Fracture for People Aged 65 and Over.* PhD Thesis, University of Sheffield.

Saal, F. E., Downey, R. G., and Lahey, M. A. (1980) Rating the ratings: Assessing the psychometric quality of rating data. *Psychological Bulletin*, 88, 413–428.

Sarno, M. T. (1993) Aphasia rehabilitation psychosocial and ethical considerations. *Aphasiology*, 7, 321–334.

Scott, J. and Huskisson, E. (1979) Vertical or horizontal visual analogue scales. *Annals of the Rheumatic Diseases*, 38, 560.

Shaw, L. and Miller, D. (2000) Defining quality healthcare with outcomes assessment while achieving economic value. *Topics in Health Information Management*, 20, 44–54.

Spitzer, W., Dobson, A., Hall, J., Chesterman, E., Levi, J., Shepherd, R., Battista, R., and Catchlove, B. (1981) Measuring quality of life of cancer patients: A concise QL-Index for use by physicians. *Journal of Chronic Diseases*, 34, 585–597.

Stephen, D. and Hetu, R. (1992) Impairment disability and handicap in audiology; towards a consensus. *Audiology*, 1–15.

Stewart, A., Hays, R., and Ware, J. (1989) The medical outcome study short form general health survey. *Medical Care*, 26, 724–733.

Streiner, D. L. and Norman, G. R. (1989) *Health Measurement Scales: A Practical Guide to their Development and Use (Chapter 8).* New York, Oxford University Press.

Swage, T. (2000) *Clinical Governance in Healthcare Practice.* Oxford, Butterworth & Heinemann.

The College of Speech and Language Therapists. (1991) *Communicating Quality: Professional Standards for Speech and Language Therapists.* Canterbury: Kent, The College of Speech and Language Therapists.

Wade, D. (1992) Measurement in neurological rehabilitation. *Current Opinion in Neurology and Neurosurgery*, 1992 October, 5(5), 682–6.

Wade, D. (2003) Outcome measures for clinical rehabilitation trials: Impairment, function, quality of life, or value? *American Journal of Physical Medicine and Rehabilitation*, 82, (10 Suppl), 26–31.

Ware, J. (1991) Measuring functioning, well-being, and other general health concepts. In Osoba, D., Ed. *Effect of Cancer on Quality of Life*, Boca Raton, CRC Press, 7–23.

Ware, J. and Sherbourne, C. (1992) The MOS 36-item Short-Form Health Survey (SF-36). Conceptual framework and item selection. *Medical Care*, 30, 473–83.

Whiteneck, S., Charlifue, S. W., Gerhart, K. A., Overholson, J. D., and Richardson, N. (1992) Quantifying handicap: A new measure of a long-term rehabilitation outcome. *Archives of Physical Medicine Rehabilitation*, 73, 519–525.

Wilkin, J., Hallam, L., and Doggett, M. (1992) *Measures of Need and Outcome for Primary Health Care*. Oxford, Oxford University Press.

Williams, A., Ware, J., and Donald, C. (1981) A model of mental health, life events and social supports applicable to general populations. *Journal of Health and Social Behaviour*, 22, 324–336.

Williams, S. J. and Bury, M. R. (1989) "Breathtaking" the consequence of chronic respiratory disorder. *International Disability Studies*, 11, 114–120.

Wood, P. H. (1980) The language of disablement: A glossary relating to disease and its consequences. *International Rehabilitation Medicine*, 2, 86–92.

Wood, P. H. N. and Badley, E. M. (1978) An epidemiological appraisal of disablement. In Bennett, A. E., Ed. *Recent advances in Community Medicine*, Edinburgh, Churchill Livingstone.

World Health Organisation. (1980) *International Classification of Impairments, Disabilities and Handicaps (ICIDH)*. Geneva, World Health Organisation.

World Health Organisation. (2001) *International Classification of Functional Disability and Health*. Geneva, World Health Organisation.

FURTHER READING

Enderby, P., Hughes, A., John, A., & Petheram, B. (2003) Using benchmark data for assessing performance in occupational therapy. *Clinical Governance: An International Journal*, 8(2), 290–295.

Enderby, P., John, A., and Sloan, M. (1995) Outcome measurement in speech and language therapy: results of a pilot study. Caring to Communicate Proceedings of the Golden Jubilee Conference York. October London, RCSLT.

Frattali, C.M. (1998) Measuring Outcomes in Speech-Language Pathology. New York; Stuttgart, Thieme.

John, A. (1998) Measuring client and carer perspectives. *International Journal of Language and Communication Disorders*, 33, 132–137.

John, A. (2002) *Therapy Outcome Measures for Benchmarking in Speech and Language Therapy*, Ph.D. Thesis, University of Sheffield.

John, A. & Enderby, P. (2000) Reliability of speech and language therapists using therapy outcome measures. *International Journal of Language and Communication Disorders*, 35, 287–302.

John, A., Enderby, P., and Sloan, M. (1995) *An outcome measure for speech and language therapists*. Proceedings of the Golden Jubilee Conference York, October, York.

John, A., Hughes, A., & Enderby, P. (2002) Establishing clinician reliability using the therapy outcome measure for the purpose of benchmarking services. *Advances in Speech-Language Pathology*, 4(2), 79–87.

Marshall, M. (2004) *A Study to Elicit the Core Components of Stroke Rehabilitation and the Subsequent Development of a Taxonomy of the Therapy Process*, PhD Thesis, Sheffield University.

Morris, M., Perry, A., Unsworth, C., Steat, J., Taylor, N., Dodd, K., Duncombe, D., & Duckett, S. (2005) Reliability of the Australian therapy outcome measures for quantifying disability and health. *International Journal of Therapy and Rehabilitation*, 12(8), 340–346.

Perry, A., Morris, M., Unsworth, C., Duckett, S., Skeat, J., Dodd, K., Taylor, N., & Reilly, K. (2004) Therapy outcome measures for allied health practitioners in Australia: the AusTOMs. *International Journal for Quality in Health Care*, 16(4), 285–291.

Radford, K., Woods, H., Lowe, D., & Rogers, S. (2004) A UK multi-centre pilot study of speech & swallowing outcomes following head and neck cancer. *Clinical Otolaryngology*, 29, 376–381.

Secretary of State for Health. (1996) The NHS: A Service with Ambitions. London, H.M.S.O.

Skeat, J. & Perry, A. (2004) Outcomes in practice: lessons from AusTOMs. *ACQuiring Knowledge in Speech, Language and Hearing*, 6(3), 123–126.

Skeat, J., Perry, A., Morris, M., Unsworth, C., Duckett, S., Dodd, K., & Taylor, N. (2003) *The Use of the ICF Framework in an Allied Health Outcome Measure: Australian Therapy Outcome Measures (AusTOMs)*. In Australian Institute of Health and Welfare (AIHW) ICF Australian User Guide. Version 1.0. Disability Series. AIHW Cat. No. DIS 33. Canberra: AIHW.

SECTION 2

Using The Tom

HOW TO CHECK THE RELIABILITY OF YOUR TEAM

The results from the reliability studies suggest that to improve consistency and stability in rating, therapists need to read the manual before using the Therapy Outcome Measure (TOM) and then practice rating some of their cases on the TOM. They should complete a rating on 10 cases with colleagues, perhaps in a team meeting, followed by rating 10 of their own cases. This practice in using the TOM and in shared rating appears to internalise the judgements on the TOM and results in consistency and stability in rating when therapists use it in a clinical context.

If a team wants to check their own reliability, they need to ensure that they conduct the trial in an appropriate manner to minimise error. The results obtained in a study of reliability can be influenced by the reliability of the reliability study itself. As random error is unpredictable, it occurs in every measure as a result of natural variations. Intervening variables can impact on the level of agreement obtained on a measure, making a reliable measure appear unreliable because of how it is used by raters/observers. Several factors have been identified that can impinge on a study and can introduce error. The following features should to be taken into consideration when planning a study:

- ***Fatigue***: the observer may become tired if the reliability study is lengthy.
- ***Motivation***: the observer may not be interested or want to do the study.
- ***Learning***: the observer may learn from doing the study.
- ***Ability***: the observer must understand the topic measured, otherwise the observer may choose a response that will make them appear better in the eyes of the tester.
- ***Skill***: the observers need to use the measure in the same way each time; their judgement should not change between subjects.
- ***Different testers***: the observer's own personality and variation in manner can influence results obtained on the measure between different observers.
- ***Environment***: different environments across time can change the observer's responses. Also, noise, heat and interruptions can intrude and affect continuity of judgement (Bailey 1997).

INTRODUCING AN OUTCOME MEASURE TO THE WORKPLACE

Before introducing an outcome measure to a service, a number of steps need to be taken so that the therapists understand not only how to use the measure itself but also how the outcome measure will be incorporated into existing data collection systems and management of the service. The measure needs to be acceptable and easy to use, and the information gained needs to be seen as of value. There needs to be a system in place to analyse the data, disseminate the result and effect action, if required.

The steps in introducing any outcome measure to a service include processes to facilitate:

- choosing the measure
- learning how to use the measure
- reliability testing
- data collection
- data analysis
- data conversion to information
- data feedback
- informing change
- managing change.

The reliability of this approach is dependent on:

- having a clear understanding of the concepts of impairment, activity, participation and well-being; you may wish to discuss these concepts with colleagues to help you become familiar with them;
- reading the manual and familiarising yourself with the specific scales;
- using the TOM to rate cases with colleagues to obtain consensus rating;
- practising rating at least in 10 patients prior to collecting reliable data; and
- team rating of cases to ensure inter-rater reliability.

Data Collection

You will need to decide which data you would like to collect information on prior to starting collection of TOM data. For example, you may want information on the individual patient/client such as age, co-morbidity, aetiology, disorder treated, location of treatment, skill-mix of the treating therapist, carer involvement, number of treatments, amount of input, duration of treatment and reason for discharge. This will help you to decide which data you need to collect on any data sheet. You may have a computerised data entry system to which the TOM data can be added, which will include the data you require on the case.

Data Feedback

The data program will produce reports on the TOM data. The authors found that it was useful for the therapists to produce data for feedback that was perceived as relevant to their work. Providing comparative tables helped the therapists to see trends within their practice, as did producing visual representations such as graphs and Pie charts.

FREQUENTLY ASKED QUESTIONS

What happens if I see my patient/client only once?
For an outcome to be measured, you need to see the person at least twice. The first time you would provide the assessment, advice and intervention. You need to have contact again to assess whether and what impact your input had. Thus, the TOM, like any other outcome measure, needs two ratings. However, if you can make two TOM ratings following one session, then do so. For example, a therapist may assess and advise and/or provide an aid or adaptation that can be classed as an intervention. The intervention can be advising on a strategy, such as modified diet, co-ordination or sequencing of activities, aids or adaptations. This may result in an immediate change in function or socialisation and should be captured in the TOM rating.

What do I do if I see the patient/client only for assessment?
The TOM is rated once an intervention is planned and treatment goals are set. A second rating is made when goals are achieved. Do not do a TOM rating if you are only completing an assessment and do not expect to have further input.

What do I do if I do not see the carer?
The carer rating is optional and should reflect the level of anxiety or concern by the carer at the start and end of treatment. It is rated only if you are providing input, which you would expect to have an impact on carer well-being.

How do I choose the ICD-10 code for the aetiology or the appropriate TOM scale when a client/patient/client has more than one?
You should use the ICD-10 code for the primary aetiology to indicate the aetiology (medical condition) underpinning the reason for referral as the first code (1) and then record the co-existing condition by coding the accompanying aetiology as ICD-10 second code (2). If there are multiple aetiologies, use the ICD-10 code to indicate the presence of multiple aetiologies. For example, someone with a learning difficulty may have a fracture or someone with Parkinson's disease might have a stroke. Page 144 provides the frequently used ICD-10 codings.

What do I do if there is more than one disorder?
You should rate the disorder (condition requiring therapy) that you are actually treating. If there is more than one disorder being treated, rate the primary disorder first under impairment 1, the other under impairment 2. If there are more than two disorders, you need to use separate TOM data rating sheets.

How do I rate activity when there is more than one disorder?
Activity concerns the overall performance of the individual. Multiple impairments affect the ability to perform tasks, for example, communicate, walk, activities of daily living. Rate the individual's overall performance. If it is important for you to record a specific activity, then use an individual data sheet to record the impairment and associated activity. You can record a second disorder code to indicate an accompanying disorder, so you will know there was a co-existing morbidity that could have influenced the final outcome (e.g. challenging behaviour and dyspraxia).

What do I do if there is no adapted scale for this condition?
You can use the TOM Core Scale (p. 84) to indicate the severity of the difficulty, limitation, disadvantage or concern.

What happens if my patient/client has variability in performance?
Patients/clients can vary in their capability to perform a task and their ability to sustain that performance. You need to make a judgement on the level of performance that the individual can achieve and sustain for most of the time. Rate the prevalent performance. For example, if an activity is observed once or only first thing in the morning, that shows capability, but you need to rate the overall performance. Rate the predominant level of performance and if the consistency of performance increases, you can reflect this at the next review.

What do I do if my patient/client has a deteriorating condition?
The TOM will show the deterioration in the impairment dimension. However, interventions may help the individual to sustain activity and participation for a time. Counselling may help support the individual emotionally and be reflected in the well-being dimension. Rating on the TOM may help you to identify how long an individual can sustain his/her activity and quality of life while the specific impairment progresses.

How do I rate patients/clients who use Environmental Aids or Augmentative Communication?
You will need to make two ratings. The first will be aided and the second will be unaided.

How do I rate a patient/client with a hearing impairment?
You will record the aetiology of hearing impairment and then you will choose the disorder most closely concerned with the reason to treat. If you are working on the activity of communication, then rate the degree of hearing impairment, first rating aided and a second rating unaided. You will then rate the ability to communicate (when aided). If you are treating another impairment, for example, articulation or

language, then you will record hearing loss under aetiology and rate the impairment you are working with as impairment 1 or 2, if more than one.

What do I do if I transfer the patient/client to another therapist?
You should provide an intermediate rating reflecting the situation before you hand over. Code this as I for intermediate and initial the entry and write in the transfer code onto the data sheet. If the patient/client is leaving your service then code the last rating as F for final and enter the discharge code for transfer to another service.

Do I rate depression under impairment or well-being?
You need to decide why you are seeing the individual. If the individual is clinically depressed, then you would record that under aetiology, and then rate the impairment that corresponds to their condition, for example, anxiety, lowness of mood. If the individual is low in spirit, because his/her mood is affected by another condition, then rate the degree of upset in the well-being dimension.

How do I analyse my data?
It all depends on what it is that you want to know. The data can be analysed in a number of ways, for example, you may wish to review a particular patient/client group or service. If the data has been entered into the TOM data analysis program then you can run a number of pre-set analyses that will provide different profiles of cases by aetiology or the disorder treated.

If you have an existing computerised management system you may wish to discuss with the responsible manager whether extra fields to capture the TOMs can be added. You might want to look at the average severity of cases entering treatment and whether this varies by age. You can then assess whether you are seeing cases when their disorder is very severe or you have fewer cases than to be expected from that population.

You might want to look at the number of cases making a change positively or negatively, or sustaining their ratings.

You might want to look at the outcome at the time of discharge from treatment and whether this varies by age, or whether the intensity or the duration of treatment is similar to that recommended in efficacy studies.

Try to think of questions that you want to answer and select the data accordingly. It is important at an early stage in implementing data collection to give serious thought to the whole process of analysis, that is, how, when and who will be involved in data analysis.

A dedicated software program, facilitating data entry and analysis, is available free of charge from Dr Brian Petheram (email brian@speech-therapy.org.uk).

TRAINING TO USE THE TOM

Summary of Local Training in Using TOM

We strongly advise that prior to using TOM, groups of staff get together to agree on certain principles of its usage and ensure that each staff member has a good understanding of the philosophical underpinning and practical issues in its application.

The group discussion may be assisted by the following format:

- Discussion regarding need for outcome measurement;
- Discussion regarding dimensions of impairment, activity, participation and well-being;
- Practice rating patients/clients (see following text for suggestions);
- Practice completing forms and coding; and
- Agreement on
  - pilot/trial study period
  - who to score (which patients/clients group – all or particular ones)
  - who/how to analyse data
  - who/how to train new staff members and
  - when to review information.

It is essential for the success of any such outcome initiative to have a clearly defined and agreed action plan that reflects the whole project.

The first training session should allow the therapists to gain a clear understanding of the underlying purpose, principles and structures of the TOM.

1. Using case studies, identify which aetiology is present and which disorder is to be treated.
2. Decide which codes to use from the code sheet or number from the ICD-10.
3. Decide which features of assessment relate to the different dimensions of impairment, activity, participation and well-being.
4. Use the Core scales to rate the case.
5. Repeat the process using the appropriate adapted scale, if available.
6. Group-practice in the use of the tool to achieve consistency in rating. For example, you could ask each member of the group to describe one of their own cases. The group then rates that case independently and then as a group. The discussion on where to rate on each dimension helps to establish consistency and stability in rating on the TOM. After rating 10 cases, the speed of completing a rating, as well as the reliability, increases.

7. Identify how to implement use of the TOM in a clinical setting.
8. Agree on action plan and dates for second group practice.

Practice on Case Studies

Therapists and nurses can practice applying the TOM scoring in different ways. One approach that we would suggest follows.

A therapist/nurse presents a case study of a patient well known to him/her. He/she should outline:

- the age
- the medical aetiology
- the condition detailing severity and complicating factors – results of any formal assessments
- what the patient/client is able/unable to do for himself/herself
- the social circumstances, social disadvantages and participation
- the emotional state
- the priorities for intervention

All other participants may ask questions to the presenter until they feel comfortable to score. The group should score the patient/client independently using the core scale and learning prompt sheet. When everyone has completed scoring, they should share the scores with the group. The participants who have attributed scores at variance with the group should explain their reasoning. It is unlikely that all those involved will agree on a precise score. But one wishes to achieve agreement by 80% of the group within one whole point. Each member then gives a further presentation in the same way but this time the persons scoring should use the detailed core scale suggested as being appropriate. This approach to training has been found to provide therapists with a familiarity and understanding of the scale. It develops consensus in judgements using the scale and develops reliability in using the measure.

Rating Practice

After the first training session, the therapists should individually rate at least ten of their own cases to develop familiarity with the scales and to increase the speed of rating.

SECOND TRAINING SESSION

The second session allows therapists to share any difficulties they have experienced in making a rating. Team rating of such cases can resolve difficulties and facilitate accurate rating between team members. A reliability check can be conducted in this session, if required.

KEY WORKER (FOR OUTCOMES)

The role of the key worker can be an important one. They should be allowed time to gain expertise and facilitate the team to implement the plan. The key worker acts as the link between the therapists and the data analysis and feedback. They can ensure that the TOM is used by all members of the service team by resolving any problems that might arise in introducing the measure and ensure new team members and locums get sufficient training and support to collect data appropriately. In addition, they can check the TOM data sheets to ensure the quality and completeness of the data returned so that valid inferences can be made from the data.

TOM SCALES

TOM Core Scales

A primary core scale reflecting the specific concepts related to the different points on the scale within each domain of impairment, activity, participation and well-being International Classification of Function/Well-being (ICF/W) allows therapists to develop specific scales related to specific client groups while maintaining the underlying principles (see Appendix VI).

The scales, reflecting the core scale principles but amplified in order to relate to the most common client groups, are presented in Appendix VII. Please note that the wording of these scales has been developed and tested in clinical situations by many therapists. However, within any profession there are different schools of thought, and whenever possible these have been accommodated; for example, is verbal dyspraxia a continuum of dysphasia/aphasia or a separate identifiable category? The scales should not "lead" the therapist but allow clinical judgement to be reflected. Therefore, if the definitions in a scale do not facilitate agreement among therapists, it is appropriate to use the general core scale or develop definitions that can be added and agreed on within a locality. In this event, it is essential to reflect on the concepts of each scale point. Rarely will everyone agree with each descriptive word, but the general philosophy and concepts should be clearly represented and users are urged to adopt them.

As described previously, the descriptors in the client-specific scales aim to achieve a method of communicating therapists' views about severity of presentation within a domain. Thus, in essence, they attempt to clarify what is meant by "severe, moderate and mild". The descriptors should prompt the therapist to help with "best match", that is, "my patient/client is most like that" if they are better or worse than the closest descriptor then the "in between" (0.5) scale point is used. Raters need to bear in mind that it is unlikely that any patient/client will fit precisely with any descriptors or have all the deficits or abilities represented in a scale description. Therapists, generally, unconsciously rank patient/clients; for example, "He is a bit better than her", "She is the worst I have seen with this disorder". The scale score attempts to assist therapists in making and clarifying these judgements.

TOM DATA SHEETS

Data Entry Form

A suggested data collection form can be found at Appendix I. Use this form if you wish to analyse the data using the companion software (available from Dr Brian Petheram – email brian@speech-therapy.org.uk). If, however, you wish to collect data by adding fields to an existing data set, you may wish to adapt the form to suit your purpose. Brief notes to help with correct completion of the forms are given in Appendix II and III.

Some additional information may be desirable according to the analyses that you wish to undertake. For example, if you wish to examine outcome measures by individual therapists, it will be necessary to enter the therapist's name on the top of the form. If you do not wish to do so, you may wish to put the profession or locality.

If you wish to analyse outcome data by date of birth, it will be necessary for you to enter on the form the age of the patient/client in years under "Patient/client Details". If you wish to analyse the information on outcomes related to the duration of treatment, you will need to fill in the treatment, duration in months, that the patient/client had achieved when the final score is detailed. The number of contacts that you have had with the patient/client should be dealt with in the same way.

It is essential that the details of these requirements be agreed on with the other therapists in your locality who are participating in the collection of outcomes. Every therapist should be completing the data form in an agreed manner. To ensure that all therapists comply over time, it is suggested that local arrangements be written down.

If you wish to have outcomes analysed according to child services or adult services, you need to identify this. This recognises that child services in different localities cover different age ranges; therefore the analysis cannot be done by age of patient/client alone.

Most outcome measure results will need grouping according to the medical and therapy diagnoses. The medical diagnosis is coded using the ICD-10 codes, for example, R13 or R13.0, and the TOM scale number that was used in rating the patient. Data entry codes for processing data on the TOM data analysis program are provided in Appendix VII. If you are analysing data locally, you may wish to amend the aetiologies or impairment codes to suit your computer program. The purpose of collecting the medical diagnosis is to capture the particular disorder that relates to the current period of treatment. That is not to say that there is no co-existing medical condition. For example, an individual with Parkinson's disease may suffer a stroke, which results in multi-factorial neurological conditions, or an individual with learning difficulties may suffer a head injury. Any co-existing condition can be noted as such.

In trials we found that many patients have more than one impairment. These can be coded on the TOM coding sheet as Code 1 or Code 2: Code 1 reflecting the primary impairment requiring intervention at this time. In a team approach each therapy group would code and rate the impairment they were targeting in treatment. For example, in the case of the patient/client with a stroke mentioned previously, the physiotherapist may code the physical impairments, the occupational therapist may code the cognitive and sensory impairments, the speech and language therapist may code the communication or dysphagic impairments and the nurse may be involved with continence.

The first assessment of the patient/client, or when he or she is admitted to treatment, should be identified with an "A" beside the first score that you undertake on a patient/client. The initial assessment of an episode of care may be arrived at after a few appointments, but should be entered prior to beginning treatment. To comply with the philosophy of this approach, which is to reflect the therapist's judgement, it is allowable to amend this initial "assessment" score if subsequent information is elicited that would clarify the clinical view; for example, the therapist may wish to lower the "A" score for well-being if a patient/client initially denies that he or she is emotionally upset by the disorder but subsequently admits to being every anxious or distressed. Place the relevant scores in the box for Impairment, Activity, Participation and Well-being. An "I" score denotes an intermediate score when you are reviewing the patient/client. There may be several "I" scores. "F" should identify the final score of an episode of care or at discharge.

If the patient/client, at any stage, has an intervening illness/event and needs a new course of therapy, a new "A" score can be used to identify this.

Well-being/Distress of Patients/Clients and Carers

Therapists (and other healthcare staff) frequently try to influence the well-being of the patients/clients and their families or caregivers. To capture information in this domain, a specific scale was developed. During the pilot studies, reported in the technical section, it became evident that it was necessary to rate the patient/client and relatives/caregivers separately and this is now accommodated on the rating form. You can rate the well-being of the client in the first space and the caregivers (if appropriate) in the second space.

Rating

Select the rating that most closely reflects the level of ability of the client. Do not forget to use 0.5 to indicate if a patient/client is slightly better or worse than a descriptor. Score two "impairment" scores if this is appropriate. The first impairment score should relate to the most relevant difficulty in this episode of care. The patient/client does not have to reflect all aspects of the description – go for the "best fit".

USER INVOLVEMENT

Determining the most appropriate way to ensure that information captures patients'/clients' and relatives' views regarding the outcome of therapy is challenging. Work has been undertaken by the authors in which patients/clients and carers have completed outcome scales with their therapists (John 1998). This involves using a semi-structured topic sheet to elicit the patient's/client's and carer's views on the level of impairment, activity, participation and well-being perceived. A vertical visual analogue rating scale (11 cm) with a range from neutral face to sad face is used by the users to rate issues raised (see Figure 2-1). This is especially helpful in identifying disadvantages in participation and concerns affecting well-being (John 1994). However, therapists do not have to adopt this approach, and this approach may not be needed in articulate users with whom the ratings at start, intermediate or final scores can be discussed. The original TOM had an agreement score which had a three-point scale that highlighted whether the user agreed with the therapist in the changes effected. The rater had to judge whether the professional/patient/client/caregiver did not agree on outcome; the professional/patient/client/caregiver did not agree equally on outcome; or the professional/patient/client/caregiver agreed on outcome in all domains. The agreement related to an agreed view even when there is no change in any domain, that is, patient, client, caregiver or professional may have total agreement that nothing has changed. However, in trials we found that therapists rarely used this agreement score, and it has been removed from the current data analysis sheet.

It may not be appropriate for a therapist to use the terms *impairment, activity, participation* and *well-being* with patients/clients and relatives. However, the information can be elicited by talking about their *specific problem*, what it *stops them from doing*, what they *are able to do*, its *effects* or *consequences on their lifestyle* and how it *affects them emotionally*. This can be done in a gentle and open way and the views of the therapist, with regard to gains, can be tested against the views of the patient/client and relatives. This approach has been found to be of value to therapists who are sometimes unaware of the different perceptions of patients/clients and relatives with regard to gains in therapy.

It is not difficult to criticise this approach to outcome measurement. Trying to capture and reflect clinical judgement in an organised and systematic way is bound to cause difficulties particularly related to subjectivity, sensitivity and reliability. However, we have published evidence that this approach holds promise; improving our collection of outcome data in a practical, reliable, achievable and communicable manner and allowing for the pooling and comparison of information related to clinical experience and different service delivery patterns.

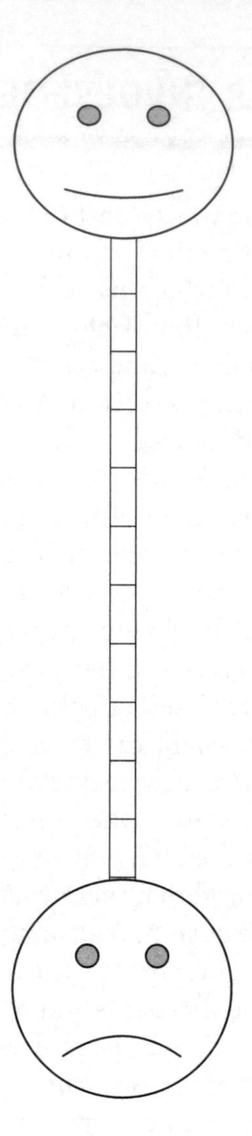

Figure 2-1. COM Scale.

THE OUTCOMES TOM COMPUTER SYSTEM

Background

The TOM software was originally developed as part of the series of research projects that created TOM as it is today. Although the TOM system can be used without involving a computer, in practical terms the use of information technology enables the TOM system's potential for the generation of high-quality information to be realised. Therefore the whole process was designed from the beginning to be suitable for computer analysis. One of the most important aspects of TOM is that it is designed to measure outcomes at the level of a service in addition to that of an individual patient. This means that analysis of data from a range of treatment episodes covering a range of cases is necessary. Also the outcomes from the service may vary according to a wide range of factors such as aetiology, amount of treatment, location of treatment and so on. This level of analysis would be possible to do "by hand" using a paper-based system but it would be slow, resource-intensive and onerous. Therefore most services that use the TOM system use a computer for storing and analysing the data and producing the reports. The actual capture is usually done by transcribing paper copies of the forms onto a computer by a data entry clerk, but because of the open nature of the software code it would be possible for suitably equipped services to adjust the system so that they can enter data directly via a portable device.

System Design

The software was originally designed as a research tool and for use only by the TOM team itself. Therefore it was put together from a variety of tools: the main software was Microsoft Visual Basic. This is a modern development environment that is object-oriented (code is developed in a modular way that facilitates flexibility and reusability) and is capable of controlling and integrating other packages such as databases and spreadsheets. In addition, it has excellent facilities for the design and production of user interfaces such as screen designs. Within the visual basic environment, use was made of Microsoft access database to store the data and Microsoft Excel spreadsheet to analyse the data and to present the reports. The software worked well and was robust. However, the software has now been re-engineered to be implemented entirely in the Microsoft Access database environment.

The rationale for re-engineering was that it became clear that the reports produced by the software were valued by the services participating in the trial and that TOM was worthy of being made more widely available. Therefore, if the software was to be routinely used by services with no support from the research team, it was necessary to ensure that the system was easy to support by using local IT support services. As well as the need to enable local support for local implementation and general maintenance (although the software is freely available, the authors are not in a position to offer IT support), the services involved in the trials all had varying needs in relation to the type of report, level of analysis and even terminology and nomenclature relating to the aetiologies and disorders. This held true within professions and between services that are ostensibly similar in terms of client group and so on. The authors took the view that it was inappropriate to attempt to use the software to enforce a spurious conformity in this regard, and therefore the software was designed in such a way that it is extremely flexible. New report types and formats can be created by the user from the screens and without any programing, and as the actual code is freely accessible – even things like report layouts and categories are able to be customised.

The software runs on any standard PC equipped with Microsoft Access database software. The TOM software itself consists of three linked modules for data entry, data management and report production. There is also a help file. The main aims of the data input module were to minimise errors and ensure that the process was as easy to use as possible. The design strategy was to develop in parallel the paper forms on which the data were recorded and the computer screen for data entry. Thus, the structure and appearance were similar in order to minimise transcription errors. Attention was paid at this stage to issues such as whether the data entry clerk would be using the numeric keypad or the main keyboard in order to speed the input of large volumes of data. The software was designed to check and validate each data item as it was entered. This was done using a variety of strategies, including specifying valid numeric ranges and using the features of the software to allow the data entry clerk to choose only from a list of valid options from a drop down list, thus minimising the chance of data entry errors.

The data are stored in the Microsoft Access database, a modern relational database system that allows completely flexible retrieval of data items. Although all the data are stored once in a single database file, it was found that useful performance gains, in terms of retrieval time, could be made by creating a range of storage structures that could be applied to the database in the form of indexes. The system enables several therapy services to be accommodated on the same system and their data can be analysed separately. The user can create or delete services as required. Data generated in the TOM format can also be imported from other systems thus facilitating cross service comparisons. As the data is stored in an Access database, the user can use all of the many Access tools such as query and report generators to analyse and present the data in any way that may be desired. However the TOM system also includes a facility to generate, create and customise reports without any knowledge of databases or programing.

The TOM software comes ready loaded with a wide range of report formats that have been found to be useful in the course of developing the system for the needs of the wide range of therapy services that were involved in the project and most users would probably find these more than adequate for their needs. However should requirements change over time or should a service wishes to analyse its data in an unforeseen way, then many parameters can be varied on screen to create new types of report. These include the name of the report, the data included, the order of the data, the type of graph or chart used to display the data and the values for the x and y axes of the charts. Reports can be viewed at any time and regenerated if new data is added to the system.

Getting and Using the Software

As can be inferred from the above, the TOM software package is a very powerful tool for capturing, analysing and presenting outcomes data. The software is currently freely available from the authors – but the authors are primarily researchers and will not be able to offer support to users of the software. This means that services that use the software will need to rely on local support. In practice this has worked well for the 100+ services in the United Kingdom and other countries that are already using the software on this basis.

The most challenging part of designing the software was finding the optimum trade-off between ease of use and the power and flexibility of the package. This has been extensively piloted and the resulting system is the fruit of extensive use and consultation. There is a manual included on the disc, and the way the software has been written with the most common software tools and with the code made accessible has meant that this form of distribution has been viable. The alternative would involve making a substantial charge for the package to cover support costs and probably the marketing of the TOM software by a professional software publisher, which would mean that the software would be as costly as other comparable specialised data analysis systems. The software has been available on this basis for some time and is widely used both in the United Kingdom and abroad (software available from Dr Brian Petheram – email brian@speech-therapy.org.uk).

REFERENCES

Bailey, D. (1997) *Research for the Health Professional: A Practical Guide* (2nd edition) F. A. Davis Co, Philadelphia.

John, A. (1994) *An Outcome Measure for Language Impaired Children Under Six Years: a Study of Reliability and Validity*, Masters Degree in Human Communication, City University, London.

John, A. (1998) Measuring client and carer perspectives. *International Journal of Language and Communication Disorders*, Special Supplement 33, 132–137.

SECTION 3

Scales and Data Forms

APPENDIX I Example of TOM Data Sheet

APPENDIX II Example of Completed Data Sheet

APPENDIX III Therapy Outcome Measures Data Form Guidance Notes

APPENDIX IV Therapy Outcome Measures Check List

APPENDIX V Learning Prompt Sheet

APPENDIX VI TOM Core Scales

APPENDIX VII Adapted Scales: Speech and Language Therapy, Physiotherapy, Occupational Therapy and Rehabilitation Nursing + Additional Scales – developed by clinicians for a specific client group

APPENDIX VIII Adapted Scales in Development

APPENDIX IX Classification of Disorders ICD-10

APPENDIX I
THERAPY OUTCOME MEASURES DATA FORM GUIDANCE NOTES

1. **Therapist's name or identifying code number**
   This information allows a checkback if data is omitted.

2. **Patients/client's/client's name/identifying code number**
   All service users can be kept anonymous but the identity code will permit checkbacks if data is missing or unclear or if some individuals have more than one form. The code can be used to extract contact and time details from the statistical system on discharge.

3. **Profession**
   Circle which profession you belong to. Data is analysed by professional groups.

4. **Employing authority**
   This identifies the employer you work for.

5. **Date of birth**
   Enter date of birth; ensure all four digits are used for the year.

6. **Carer**
   Identify which carer is being rated, for example, mother, spouse, family unit, key worker

7. **Aetiology codes**
   You may use the ICD-10 codes or you can select a code from the coding sheet. These codes are used in the TOM data analysis programme. Note that certain aetiologies have multiple features as part of the condition. Some clients may have a multifactorial condition, involving more than one aetiology relating to the reason for seeing them, in that case rate the primary aetiology relating to the reason for the referral first (1) and rate the other or the longer standing existing condition as the second aetiology (2). If there are multiple aetiologies use code "Multifactorial".

8. **Disorder codes**
   Select the code from the sheet to indicate what is being treated and enter this as Impairment Code 1, if there are two separate disorders, that is, if the patient/client has more than one disorder, then rate the most relevant disorder first as Impairment Code 1 and the second as Impairment Code 2. For each code rated note which TOM rating sheet was used. For certain disorders you may need to use a second sheet.

9. **Rating**
   Admission (A): Detail the outcome score for the patient/client when you are starting treatment for the first time. Record the date rated.

   Intermediate (I): If you alter treatment or have ended an episode of care, but are not discharging the patient/client, enter an intermediate rating. For patients/clients in long-term intervention a rating may be completed at a set period to fit in with reviews.

   Final (F): Rate the patient/client at the end of treatment on discharge from intervention. If the patient/client suffers an incident, which dramatically changes their profile (e.g. second stroke) then give them a final rating, give a discharge code stating the reason for terminating this period of intervention, and then open a new form to reflect the new circumstances.

   Well-being: Always rate the well-being of the patient/client/carer in the first box, and rate of the carer (when relevant) in the second box.

   Select the score most closely representing your patient's/client's/carer's ability, they may not be exactly as the descriptor suggests, choose the one of "best fit" and remember that not all the descriptors apply. The descriptors are to facilitate rating on each domain of the measure. Use half-points to indicate whether someone is slightly better or worse than a particular score point. If there are two impairments rate both, if one is more relevant to the episode of care, rate this first as the primary one.

10. **Number of contacts**
    Complete with details of all patient/client related contacts. Patient/client related activity is any activity that contributes to the care of an individual named client who is registered on the caseload of the department.

This includes non – face-to-face contacts as patient/client related activity. If possible obtain this information from the statistical records.

11. **Total time**
Complete details of the time spent on patient/client/carer activities. If possible obtain this information from the statistical records.

12. **Discharges**
Enter the reason for the discharge in the space on the sheet. You can use the codes provided.

13. **Comments**
This area is available to provide qualitative information. You may wish to record specific information or concerns. Ratings may not reflect real change or be difficult to reflect for that individual.

APPENDIX II
THERAPY OUTCOME MEASURES DATA COLLECTION SHEET

Therapist identity/code :
Patient/client Identity :
(Name or Code Number)
N.B. This information is for local use and will be removed before the Data Sheet leaves the Service

Employing Authority :____

Locality :____________________

Profession : Speech and Language Therapy, Physiotherapy,Occupational Therapy, Rehabilitation Nursing, Hearing Therapists

Patient/client/Client Details

Age at Entry

Date of Birth : ____/____/______ (dd mm yyyy) **Carer :**____________________(person rated)

Aetiology Code 1 : _______ _______ **Aetiology Code 2 :** _______ _______

Impairment Code 1 : _______ _______ **TOM scale used :**

Impairment Code 2 : _______ _______ **TOM scale used :**

Ratings

Code*	Impairment Code 1	Impairment Code 2	Activity	Social Participation	Well-being Patient/client	Well-being Carer	Date Rated
A-							
I-							

* A = Admission to therapy, First rating : I = Intermediate ratings (when placed at the first entry it denotes previous interventions from therapy) F = Final rating.

Number of Contacts :________ **Total time :** _______hrs______mins **Discharge Code** _______

Comments :____

Please send this form to your key worker for checking and data entry.

APPENDIX III
EXAMPLE OF COMPLETED DATA SHEET

Therapist identity/code :
Patient/client Identity : JAMES BOND 007
(Name or Code Number)

Employing Authority : ANYWHERE PCT
Locality : PT outpatient/client clinic

Profession : Speech and Language Therapy, (Physiotherapy,) Occupational Therapy, Rehabilitation Nursing, Hearing Therapists

Patient/client/Client Details

Age at Entry
Date of Birth : 06/ 10/ 1959
dd mm yyyy

Carer : SPOUSE (person rated)

Aetiology Code 1 : M 25 **Aetiology Code 2 :** R 62.0

Impairment Code 1 : M 62.9 **TOM Rating Sheet :** Musculo-skeletal

Impairment Code 2 : R 52 **TOM Rating Sheet :** Core Scale used to rate Pain

Ratings

Code*	Impairment Code1	Impairment Code 2	Activity	Social Participation	Well-being Patient/client	Well-being Carer	Date Rated
A-	1	3	2	3	3	2	12 / 06 /04
I-	3	4	3.5	4	4	3	06 / 09 /04
F	4.5	5	4	4	4	4	08 / 12 /04

* **A** = Admission to therapy, First rating : **I** = Intermediate ratings (when placed at the first entry it denotes previous interventions from therapy); **F** = Final rating.

Number of Contacts : 21 **Total time :** 12 hrs 30 mins **Discharge Code:** R2

Use R0 if analysing rating but case is not discharged

Comments : ____________________

Please send this form to your key worker for checking and data entry.

APPENDIX IV
THERAPY OUTCOME MEASURES CHECK LIST

- ***What is the aim of using the Therapy Outcome Measures?***
The aim is to assess entry points and exit points from treatment; to note change and resources associated with change.

- ***Who to rate?***
Rate all new patient/clients (and their carers if appropriate) entering an episode of care (A). Rate long-term cases at the start of their next episode of care with an intermediate care (I).

- ***When to rate?***
Rate after the assessment, when you have gathered the relevant case history, the assessment data, when you are ready to start treatment, and before you start the treatment programme.
Rate at the end of an episode of care (I) and/or at discharge (F).
Rate those in maintenance or continuing care at review points (I).
An episode of care is defined as a period of treatment working towards achieving the goals of treatment. A new episode of care begins when the goals of treatment are changed.

- ***When to give final rating?***
Give a final score (F) at the time of discharge from your service.
If the individual's condition is compromised by another but separate health incident, such as a fracture or has another stroke, then give the individual a final (F) score and indicate under comments the reason for "final" rating is a change in condition and start a new form as for a new patient/client. If the individual was discharged from care because they "Did Not Attend" (DNA), then rate the individual as they were when they were last seen with a (F) score and use record the reason for discharge (DNA). If the individual is discharged

following a telephone check then a discharge rating can be made, provided there is information to rate all dimensions of the Therapy Outcome Measures (TOM). Remember to complete contacts, time and discharge code. Spaces not completed on the form will result in the patient/client entry not being analysed on the TOM data analysis programme.

- ***What to do with the completed form?***
  Send the completed form to your key worker or designated data clerk or manager.

APPENDIX V
LEARNING PROMPT SHEET

IMPAIRMENT

Each team member should rate the severity of the presentation of the disorder as it affects the person's capacities (*for their age*) in their specific area (e.g. gross motor skills, physical deficit, language, cognitive, psychological disorder).

Very Severe	Severe	Severe/Moderate	Moderate	Mild	No Impairment
0/0.5	**1/1.5**	**2/2.5**	**3/3.5**	**4/4.5**	**5**

ACTIVITY

Each team member should rate the degree to which a person's impairment affects their ability to perform a task/function *at an age-appropriate level* (e.g. mobility, dexterity, communication, self-feeding, learning, independence, appropriateness of emotional responses, behaviour).

Unable to perform task/totally dependant on others/no awareness of surroundings	Assists/ co-operates but burden of task falls on carers/ awareness of surroundings	Can undertake some part of task but needs a high level of support to complete/ some interaction with environment	Can undertake task/function/ interaction in familiar situation but need some verbal/physical assistance at other times	Requires some minor assistance occasion-ally or extra time to complete task	Age- appro-priately/ independent/ able to func-tion/perform task/interacts with environment appropriately
0/0.5	**1/1.5**	**2/2.5**	**3/3.5**	**4/4.5**	**5**

PARTICIPATION

The whole team should rate the degree to which a person's impairment affects their (age related) functioning within a social context/the family, that is, ability to make choices and have control over their lives/environment; self-awareness and confidence; integration into age-appropriate activities; achievement of potential. This dimension reflects the capabilities of the patient/client as well as the environment and those in the environment.

Isolated, no control over environment, no relationships, unable to exercise choice "too protected"/ total control in family	Very limited choices, little control over life, some awareness of self within environment, very abnormal role/control	Able to make some choices, able to access non-integrated facilities, moderately abnormal role in family/ environment	Some supported integration, achievement of potential with encouragement, some control over life, some abnormal control/role	Mostly confident, occasionally some restriction in integration or lack of confidence	Integrated, valued and autonomous in family and society
0/0.5	**1/1.5**	**2/2.5**	**3/3.5**	**4/4.5**	**5**

WELL-BEING

The team should rate the degree of upset affecting the person/carers (2 scores)*

Severe consistent distress, complete detachment – no appropriate emotions	Severe consistent distress frequently experienced; mainly detached	Moderate consistent distress, severe occasional distress, frequent detachment	Moderate distress frequently experienced, often inappropriately detached	Distress occasionally experienced, occasional inappropriate detachment	Not inappropriate distress/ detachment
0/0.5	**1/1.5**	**2/2.5**	**3/3.5**	**4/4.5**	**5**

* Do not try to attribute distress to any aspect of the person's life or difficulties. Rate this overall even if you think the degree of upset is related to some extraneous issue, e.g. finances/housing, etc.

APPENDIX VI
TOM CORE SCALE

Identify descriptor that is "best fit". The patient/client does not have to have each feature mentioned. Use 0.5 to indicate if the patient/client is slightly better or worse than a descriptor and as appropriate to age.

IMPAIRMENT

0 The most severe presentation of this impairment
1 Severe presentation of this impairment
2 Severe/moderate presentation
3 Moderate presentation
4 Just below normal/mild impairment
5 No impairment

ACTIVITY

0 Totally dependent/unable to function
1 Assists/co-operates but burden of task/achievement falls on professional or caregiver.
2 Can undertake some part of task but needs a high level of support to complete
3 Can undertake task/function in familiar situation but requires some verbal/physical assistance
4 Requires some minor assistance occasionally or extra time to complete task
5 Independent/able to function

PARTICIPATION

0 No autonomy, isolated, no social/family life
1 Very limited choices, contact mainly with professionals, no social or family role, little control over life
2 Some integration, value and autonomy in one setting
3 Integrated, valued and autonomous in limited number of settings
4 Occasionally some restriction in autonomy, integration or role
5 Integrated, valued, occupies appropriate role

WELL-BEING/DISTRESS

0 **Severe constant:** High and constant levels of distress/upset/concern/frustration/anger/distress/embarrassment/withdrawal/severe depression/or apathy, unable to express or control emotions appropriately.

1 **Frequently severe:** Moderate distress/upset/concern/frustration/anger/distress/embarrassment/withdrawal/severe depression/or apathy. Becomes concerned easily, requires constant reassurance/support, needs clear/tight limits and structure, loses emotional control easily.

2 **Moderate consistent:** Distress/upset/concern/frustration/anger/distress/embarrassment/withdrawal/severe depression/or apathy in unfamiliar situations, frequent emotional encouragement and support required.

3 **Moderate frequent:** Distress/upset/concern/frustration/anger/distress/embarrassment/withdrawal/severe depression/or apathy. Controls emotions with assistance, emotionally dependent on some occasions, vulnerable to change in routine, etc., spontaneously uses methods to assist emotional control.

4 **Mild occasional:** Distress/upset/concern/frustration/anger/distress/embarrassment/withdrawal/severe depression/or apathy. Able to control feelings in most situations, generally well adjusted/stable (most of the time/most situations), occasional emotional support/encouragement needed.

5 **Not inappropriate:** Distress/upset/concern/frustration/anger/distress/embarrassment/withdrawal/severe depression/or apathy. Well-adjusted, stable and able to cope emotionally with most situations, good insight, accepts and understands own limitations.

APPENDIX VII
THERAPY OUTCOME MEASURES ADAPTED SCALES

1 CHILD SPEECH/LANGUAGE IMPAIRMENT
2 PHONOLOGICAL DISORDER
3 DYSARTHRIA
4 DYSFLUENCY
5 DYSPHAGIA
6 DYSPHASIA/APHASIA
7 DYSPHONIA
8 HEARING THERAPY/AURAL REHABILITATION
9 LARYNGECTOMY
10 LEARNING DISABILITY (COMMUNICATION)
11 DYSPRAXIA (CHILDREN WITH DEVELOPMENTAL CO-ORDINATION DIFFICULTIES)
12 CEREBRAL PALSY
13 COGNITION
14 HEAD INJURY
15 STROKE
16 NEUROLOGICAL DISORDERS
17 COMPLEX AND MULTIPLE DIFFICULTY
18 CARDIAC REHABILITATION
19 MULTI-FACTORIAL CONDITIONS
20 MUSCULO-SKELETAL
21 RESPIRATORY CARE (COPD)

1. CHILD SPEECH/LANGUAGE IMPAIRMENT

Identify descriptor that is "best fit". The patient/client does not have to have each feature mentioned. Use 0.5 to indicate if patient/client is slightly better or worse than a descriptor and as appropriate to age.

IMPAIRMENT

0 **Profound language impairment:** Profound problems are evident in all areas, extremely limited language involving use, comprehension, expression and phonology.

1 **Severe language impairment:** Severe problems usually involving all areas, severe problems in two or more areas, one profound overriding area involving use, comprehension, expression and phonology.

2 **Severe/moderate language impairment:** Severe/moderate problems in some areas may involve one severe overriding area involving use, comprehension, expression and phonology.

3 **Moderate language impairment:** Moderate problems in some areas and/or specific moderate problems in one area of language involving use, comprehension, expression, phonology.

4 **Mild impairment:** Mild problems in one or more areas involving use, comprehension, expression, phonology. Delay sufficient to involve monitoring.

5 **No impairment:** Age-appropriate language in all areas.

ACTIVITY

0 Unable to communicate in any way. No effective understanding even in context.

1 Occasionally able to make basic needs known and able to follow simple instructions in context; can only do this with a trained listener in familiar settings. Minimal communication with maximal assistance.

2 Consistently able to make basic needs known and able to follow simple instructions in context. Communicates better with a trained listener and family members but can occasionally communicate with people that he or she does not know in familiar settings. Depends heavily on context and cues.

3 Consistently able to make needs known but can occasionally convey more information than this. Able to follow most of a conversation in context; can communicate with familiar people or strangers in some unfamiliar as well as familiar settings. Needs some cues and patient/client assistance or extra time.

4 Occasional difficulties experienced in effective communication; may have some difficulty with certain people or in specific situations.

5 Communicates well in all situations; age appropriate.

PARTICIPATION

0 Unable to fulfil any social/educational/family role. Not involved in decision-making/no autonomy/no control over environment, no social integration.

1 Low self-confidence/poor self-esteem/limited social integration/socially isolated/contributes to some basic and limited decisions. Cannot achieve potential in any situation.

2 Some self-confidence/some social integration/makes some decisions and influences control in familiar situations.

3 Some self-confidence; autonomy emerging. Makes decisions and has control of some aspects of life. Able to achieve some limited social integration/educational activities. Diffident over control over life. Needs encouragement to achieve potential.

4 Mostly confident; occasional difficulties integrating or in fulfilling social/role activity. Participating in all appropriate decisions. May have difficulty in achieving potential in some situations occasionally.

5 Achieving potential. Autonomous and unrestricted. Able to fulfil social, educational and family role.

WELL-BEING/DISTRESS

0 **Severe constant:** High and constant levels of distress/upset/concern/frustration/anger/distress/embarrassment/withdrawal/severe depression or apathy, unable to express or control emotions appropriately.

1 **Frequently severe:** Moderate distress/upset/concern/frustration/anger/distress/embarrassment/withdrawal/severe depression or apathy. Becomes concerned easily, requires constant reassurance/support, needs clear/tight limits and structure, loses emotional control easily.

2 **Moderate consistent:** Distress/upset/concern/frustration/anger/distress/embarrassment/withdrawal/severe depression or apathy in unfamiliar situations, frequent emotional encouragement and support required.

3 **Moderate frequent:** Distress/upset/concern/frustration/anger/distress/embarrassment/withdrawal/severe depression or apathy. Controls emotions with assistance, emotionally dependant on some occasions, vulnerable to change in routine, etc., spontaneously uses methods to assist emotional control.

4 **Mild occasional:** Distress/upset/concern/frustration/anger/distress/embarrassment/withdrawal/severe depression or apathy. Able to control feelings in most situations, generally well adjusted/stable (most of the time/most situations), occasional emotional support/encouragement needed.

5 **Not inappropriate:** Distress/upset/concern/frustration/anger/distress/embarrassment/withdrawal/severe depression or apathy. Well adjusted, stable and able to cope emotionally with most situations, good insight, accepts and understands own limitations.

2. PHONOLOGICAL DISORDER

Identify descriptor that is "best fit". The patient/client does not have to have each feature mentioned. Use 0.5 to indicate if patient/client is slightly better or worse than a descriptor and as appropriate to age.

IMPAIRMENT

0 Totally limited sound system; uses no recognisable consonants.

1 Speech system restricted; uses a few recognisable sounds including some consonants.

2 Good use of consonants and vowels at single word level but poor transfer of sounds into sentences. May have 25% to 50% suppression of inappropriate processes.

3 Capable of clear speech when thinking about it and prompted, but clarity deteriorates in spontaneous speech. May have 50% to 75% suppression of inappropriate processes.

4 Persistent minor immaturities; may have typical processes at a later age or one atypical process.

5 Age-appropriate speech.

ACTIVITY

0 Completely unintelligible to familiar and non-familiar listeners.

1 Partly intelligible to familiar listeners in known context; communication partner bears the burden of the responsibility.

2 Intelligible to familiar listeners in context; partly intelligible in context with non-familiar listeners; single words clear, connected speech poor.

3 Usually intelligible to familiar listeners in and out of context; variable intelligibility in context with non-familiar listeners; free, spontaneous speech often unintelligible.

4 Minor problems but intelligible to every one; occasionally loses intelligibility at times, for example when excited or speaking against noise, etc.

5 Intelligible at age-appropriate level to familiar listeners and non-familiar listeners.

PARTICIPATION

0 Unable to fulfil any social/educational/family role. Not involved in decision-making/no autonomy/no control over environment, no social integration.

1 Low self-confidence/poor self-esteem/limited social integration/socially isolated/contributes to some basic and limited decisions. Cannot achieve potential in any situation.

2 Some self-confidence/some social integration/makes some decisions and influences control in familiar situations.

3 Some self-confidence; autonomy emerging. Makes decisions and has control of some aspects of life. Able to achieve some limited social integration/educational activities. Diffident over control over life. Needs encouragement to achieve potential.

4 Mostly confident; occasional difficulties integrating or in fulfilling social/role activity. Participating in all appropriate decisions. May have difficulty in achieving potential in some situations occasionally.

5 Achieving potential. Autonomous and unrestricted. Able to fulfil social, educational and family role.

WELL-BEING/DISTRESS

0 **Severe constant:** High and constant levels of distress/upset/concern/frustration/anger/distress/embarrassment/withdrawal/severe depression or apathy, unable to express or control emotions appropriately.

1 **Frequently severe:** Moderate distress/upset/concern/frustration/anger/distress/embarrassment/withdrawal/severe depression or apathy. Becomes concerned easily, requires constant reassurance/support, needs clear/tight limits and structure, loses emotional control easily.

2 **Moderate consistent:** Distress/upset/concern/frustration/anger/distress/embarrassment/withdrawal/severe depression or apathy in unfamiliar situations, frequent emotional encouragement and support required.

3 **Moderate frequent:** Distress/upset/concern/frustration/anger/distress/embarrassment/withdrawal/severe depression or apathy. Controls emotions with assistance, emotionally dependant on some occasions, vulnerable to change in routine, etc., spontaneously uses methods to assist emotional control.

4 **Mild occasional:** Distress/upset/concern/frustration/anger/distress/embarrassment/withdrawal/severe depression or apathy. Able to control feelings in most situations, generally well adjusted/stable (most of the time/most situations), occasional emotional support/encouragement needed.

5 **Not inappropriate:** Distress/upset/concern/frustration/anger/distress/embarrassment/withdrawal/severe depression or apathy. Well adjusted, stable and able to cope emotionally with most situations, good insight, accepts and understands own limitations.

3. DYSARTHRIA

Identify descriptor that is "best fit". The patient/client does not have to have each feature mentioned. Use 0.5 to indicate if patient/client is slightly better or worse than a descriptor and as appropriate to age.

IMPAIRMENT

0 **Severe dysarthria:** severe persistent articulatory/prosodic impairment. Inability to produce any distinguishable speech sounds. No oral motor control. No respiratory support for speech.

1 **Severe/moderate dysarthria:** with consistent articulatory/prosodic impairment. Mostly open vowel sounds with some consonant approximations/severe festination of speech. Extremely effortful or slow speech; only 1 or 2 words per breath. Severely limited motor control.

2 **Moderate dysarthria:** with frequent episodes of articulatory/prosodic impairment. Most consonants attempted but poorly represented acoustically/moderate festination. Very slow speech; manages up to 4 words per breath. Moderate limitation oral motor control.

3 **Moderate/mild dysarthria:** consistent omission/articulation of consonants. Variability of speed. Mild limitation of oral motor control or prosodic impairment.

4 **Mild dysarthria:** slight or occasional omission/mispronunciation of consonants. Slight or occasional difficulty with oral motor control/prosody or respiratory support.

5 **No Impairment**.

ACTIVITY

0 Unable to communicate in any way. No effective communication. No interaction.

1 Occasionally able to make basic needs known with familiar persons or trained listeners in familiar contexts. Minimal communication with maximal assistance

2 Limited functional communication. Consistently able to make basic needs/conversation understood but is heavily dependent on cues and context. Communicates better with trained listener or family members or in familiar settings. Frequent repetition required. Maintained meaningful interaction related to here and now.

3 Consistently able to make needs known but can sometimes convey more information than this. Some inconsistency in unfamiliar settings. Is less dependant for intelligibility on cues and context. Occasional repetition required. Communicates beyond here/now with familiar persons, needs some cues and prompting.

4 Can be understood most of the time by any listener despite communication irregularities. Holds conversation; requires special consideration, for example, patience, time, attention, especially with a wider range of people.

5 Communicates effectively in all situations.

PARTICIPATION

0 Unable to fulfil any social/educational/family role. Not involved in decision-making/no autonomy/no control over environment, no social integration.

1 Low self-confidence/poor self-esteem/limited social integration/socially isolated/contributes to some basic and limited decisions. Cannot achieve potential in any situation.

2 Some self-confidence/some social integration/makes some decisions and influences control in familiar situations.

3 Some self-confidence; autonomy emerging. Makes decisions and has control of some aspects of life. Able to achieve some limited social integration/educational activities. Diffident over control over life. Needs encouragement to achieve potential.

4 Mostly confident; occasional difficulties integrating or in fulfilling social/role activity. Participating in all appropriate decisions. May have difficulty in achieving potential in some situations occasionally.

5 Achieving potential. Autonomous and unrestricted. Able to fulfil social, educational and family role.

WELL-BEING/DISTRESS

0 **Severe constant:** High and constant levels of distress/upset/concern/frustration/anger/distress/embarrassment/withdrawal/severe depression or apathy, unable to express or control emotions appropriately.

1 **Frequently severe:** Moderate distress/upset/concern/frustration/anger/distress/embarrassment/withdrawal/severe depression or apathy. Becomes concerned easily, requires constant reassurance/support, needs clear/tight limits and structure, loses emotional control easily.

2 **Moderate consistent:** Distress/upset/concern/frustration/anger/distress/embarrassment/withdrawal/severe depression or apathy in unfamiliar situations, frequent emotional encouragement and support required.

3 **Moderate frequent:** Distress/upset/concern/frustration/anger/distress/embarrassment/withdrawal/severe depression or apathy. Controls emotions with assistance, emotionally dependent on some occasions, vulnerable to change in routine, etc., spontaneously uses methods to assist emotional control.

4 **Mild occasional:** Distress/upset/concern/frustration/anger/distress/embarrassment/withdrawal/severe depression or apathy. Able to control feelings in most situations, generally well adjusted/stable (most of the time/most situations), occasional emotional support/encouragement needed.

5 **Not inappropriate:** Distress/upset/concern/frustration/anger/distress/embarrassment/withdrawal/severe depression or apathy. Well adjusted, stable and able to cope emotionally with most situations, good insight, accepts and understands own limitations.

4. DYSFLUENCY

Identify descriptor that is "best fit". The patient/client does not have to have each feature mentioned. Use 0.5 to indicate if patient/client is slightly better or worse than a descriptor and as appropriate to age.

IMPAIRMENT

0 **Severe stammer:** Examples of behaviour: tension-associated gestures and behaviours, many repetitions, long prolongations, marked and repeated blocks; frequent avoidance of many words, stammer always evident.

1 **Severe/moderate stammer:** Examples of behaviour: blocks, fairly long prolongations, some tension-associated behaviours and gestures, occasional associated gestures and behaviours; frequent avoidance of some words, stammer frequently evident and severe stammer behaviours occurring occasionally.

2 **Moderate stammering:** Examples of behaviour: blocks, short prolongations, repetitions, some tension-associated behaviours and gestures; occasional avoidance of a few words, stammer sometimes evident or severe/moderate stammer occurring occasionally.

3 **Moderate/slight stammer:** Examples of behaviour: occasional prolongations, repetitions, slight tension; occasional avoidance of specific words, stammer sometimes evident or moderate stammer occurring occasionally.

4 **Slight stammer:** Examples of behaviour: easy repetitions; stammer occasionally evident or moderate stammer or avoidance occurring infrequently.

5 **No stammer.**

ACTIVITY

0 Interaction severely disrupted at all times. Great difficulty getting message across to any listener.

1 Interaction severely disrupted with less familiar listeners in most situations, occasionally less disrupted with familiar listeners. Significant difficulty getting message across to listeners. Avoids many situations and people.

2 Interaction moderately disrupted with some listeners or in several different situations, less disrupted with other listeners/some difficulty getting message across to listener/marked variability. Avoids some situations and people.

3 Interaction slightly disrupted with some listeners or situations, less disrupted with other listeners/slight difficulty getting message across to listener/less variability. Avoids occasional situations and people.

4 Interaction occasionally disrupted with some listeners or in occasional specific situations; no problems with other listeners/very occasional and slight difficulty getting message across to listener. Does not avoid situations or people.

5 No disruption to communication. No difficulty getting message across to listener.

PARTICIPATION

0 Unable to fulfil any social/educational/family role. Not involved in decision-making/no autonomy/no control over environment, no social integration.

1 Low self-confidence/poor self-esteem/limited social integration/socially isolated/contributes to some basic and limited decisions. Cannot achieve potential in any situation.

2 Some self-confidence/some social integration/makes some decisions and influences control in familiar situations.

3 Some self-confidence; autonomy emerging. Makes decisions and has control of some aspects of life. Able to achieve some limited social integration/educational activities. Diffident over control over life. Needs encouragement to achieve potential.

4 Mostly confident; occasional difficulties integrating or in fulfilling social/role activity. Participating in all appropriate decisions. May have difficulty in achieving potential in some situations occasionally.

5 Achieving potential. Autonomous and unrestricted. Able to fulfil social, educational and family role.

WELL-BEING/DISTRESS

0 **Severe constant:** High and constant levels of distress/upset/concern/frustration/anger/distress/embarrassment/withdrawal/severe depression or apathy, unable to express or control emotions appropriately.

1 **Frequently severe:** Moderate distress/upset/concern/frustration/anger/distress/embarrassment/withdrawal/severe depression or apathy. Becomes concerned easily, requires constant reassurance/support, needs clear/tight limits and structure, loses emotional control easily.

2 **Moderate consistent:** Distress/upset/concern/frustration/anger/distress/embarrassment/withdrawal/severe depression or apathy in unfamiliar situations, frequent emotional encouragement and support required.

3 **Moderate frequent:** Distress/upset/concern/frustration/anger/distress/embarrassment/withdrawal/severe depression or apathy. Controls emotions with assistance, emotionally dependent on some occasions, vulnerable to change in routine, etc., spontaneously uses methods to assist emotional control.

4 **Mild occasional:** Distress/upset/concern/frustration/anger/distress/embarrassment/withdrawal/severe depression or apathy. Able to control feelings in most situations, generally well adjusted/stable (most of the time/most situations), occasional emotional support/encouragement needed.

5 **Not inappropriate:** Distress/upset/concern/frustration/anger/distress/embarrassment/withdrawal/severe depression or apathy. Well adjusted, stable and able to cope emotionally with most situations, good insight, accepts and understands own limitations.

5. DYSPHAGIA

Identify descriptor that is "best fit". The patient/client does not have to have each feature mentioned. Use 0.5 to indicate if patient/client is slightly better or worse than a descriptor and as appropriate to age.

IMPAIRMENT

0 **Aphagia:** Not safe to swallow due to cognitive status/no bolus control/aspiration/absence of oral/pharyngeal swallow. Clinical signs of aspiration. No cough reflex. May need regular suction.

1 **Severe dysphagia:** Weak oral movements/no bolus control/inadequate/inconsistent swallow reflex. High risk of aspiration.

2 **Severe/moderate dysphagia:** Cough/swallow reflexes evident but abnormal or delayed. Uncoordinated oral movements. Risk of aspiration.

3 **Moderate dysphagia:** Swallow and cough reflex present. May have poor oral control. At risk of occasional aspiration.

4 **Mild oral/pharyngeal dysphagia:** incoordination but no clinical evidence of aspiration

5 **No evidence of dysphagia.**

ACTIVITY

0 Non-oral feeding to meet all hydration and nutritional needs. Variable ability to take practice amounts of modified consistencies using compensatory strategies. Some management of sections. Needs experienced supervision.

1 Non-oral feeding to meet all hydration and nutritional needs. Variable ability to take practice amounts of modified consistencies using compensatory strategies. Some management of secretions. Needs experienced supervision.

2 Non-oral feeding/supplements needed to meet hydration and nutritional needs. Consistently able to take practice amount of modified consistencies using compensatory strategies. Needs experienced supervision.

3 Consistently able to take modified consistencies using compensatory strategies. Needs some supervision, may require feeding supplements, may eat extremely slowly.

4 Although eating and drinking is abnormal, it is good enough to meet nutritional requirements. No supervision required. No alternative or supplement feeding. May avoid certain foods, drinks, or eating situations.

5 Functionally eating and drinking a normal diet.

PARTICIPATION

0 Unable to fulfil any social/educational/family role. Not involved in decision-making/no autonomy/no control over environment, no social integration.

1 Low self-confidence/poor self-esteem/limited social integration/socially isolated/contributes to some basic and limited decisions. Cannot achieve potential in any situation.

2 Some self-confidence/some social integration/makes some decisions and influences control in familiar situations.

3 Some self-confidence; autonomy emerging. Makes decisions and has control of some aspects of life. Able to achieve some limited social integration/educational activities. Diffident over control over life. Needs encouragement to achieve potential.

4 Mostly confident; occasional difficulties integrating or in fulfilling social/role activity. Participating in all appropriate decisions. May have difficulty in achieving potential in some situations occasionally.

5 Achieving potential. Autonomous and unrestricted. Able to fulfil social, educational and family role.

WELL-BEING/DISTRESS

0 **Severe constant:** High and constant levels of distress/upset/concern/frustration/anger/distress/embarrassment/withdrawal/severe depression or apathy, unable to express or control emotions appropriately.

1 **Frequently severe:** Moderate distress/upset/concern/frustration/anger/distress/embarrassment/withdrawal/severe depression or apathy. Becomes concerned easily, requires constant reassurance/support, needs clear/tight limits and structure, loses emotional control easily.

2 **Moderate consistent:** Distress/upset/concern/frustration/anger/distress/embarrassment/withdrawal/severe depression or apathy in unfamiliar situations, frequent emotional encouragement and support required.

3 **Moderate frequent:** Distress/upset/concern/frustration/anger/distress/embarrassment/withdrawal/severe depression or apathy. Controls emotions with assistance, emotionally dependent on some occasions, vulnerable to change in routine, etc., spontaneously uses methods to assist emotional control.

4 **Mild occasional:** Distress/upset/concern/frustration/anger/distress/embarrassment/withdrawal/severe depression or apathy. Able to control feelings in most situations, generally well adjusted/stable (most of the time/most situations), occasional emotional support/encouragement needed.

5 **Not inappropriate:** Distress/upset/concern/frustration/anger/distress/embarrassment/withdrawal/severe depression or apathy. Well adjusted, stable and able to cope emotionally with most situations, good insight, accepts and understands own limitations.

6. DYSPHASIA/APHASIA

Identify descriptor that is "best fit". The patient/client does not have to have each feature mentioned. Use 0.5 to indicate if patient/client is slightly better or worse than a descriptor and as appropriate to age.

IMPAIRMENT

0 **Aphasia affecting all modalities:** Auditory and reading comprehension inconsistent even at one keyword. No meaningful expression.

1 **Severe dysphasia/aphasia:** Auditory and/or reading comprehension is consistent at one keyword level. Occasionally understand and expresses limited amount.

2 **Severe/moderate dysphasia/aphasia:** Auditory and/or reading comprehension consistent at a minimum of two or three keyword level. Some limited verbal and/or written expression used appropriately and purposefully.

3 **Moderate dysphasia/aphasia:** Constant auditory and/or reading comprehension for simple sentences or structures. Inconsistent with complex commands and structures. Consistently reduced verbal and/or written language structure and vocabulary. May have a specific more severe difficulty in one modality.

4 **Mild dysphasia/aphasia:** Occasional difficulties present in auditory and/or reading comprehension and in verbal and/or written expression.

5 **No dysphasia/aphasia.**

ACTIVITY

0 Unable to communicate in any way. No effective communication. No interaction.

1 Occasionally able to make basic needs known with familiar persons or trained listeners in familiar contexts. Minimal communication with maximal assistance.

2 Limited functional communication. Consistently able to make basic needs/conversation understood but is heavily dependent on cues and context. Communicates better with trained listener or family members or in familiar settings. Frequent repetition required. Maintains meaningful interaction related to here and now.

3 Consistently able to make needs known but can sometimes convey more information than this. Some inconsistency in unfamiliar settings. Is less dependent for intelligibility on cues and context. Occasional repetition required. Communicates beyond here/now with familiar persons; needs cues and prompting.

4 Can be understood most of the time by any listener despite communication irregularities. Holds conversation; requires occasional prompts particularly with a wider range of people.

5 Communicates effectively in all situations.

PARTICIPATION

0 Unable to fulfil any social/educational/family role. Not involved in decision-making/no autonomy/no control over environment; no social integration.

1 Low self-confidence/poor self-esteem/limited social integration/socially isolated/contributes to some basic and limited decisions. Cannot achieve potential in any situation.

2 Some self-confidence/some social integration/makes some decisions and influences control in familiar situations.

3 Some self-confidence; autonomy emerging. Makes decisions and has control of some aspects of life. Able to achieve some limited social integration/educational activities. Diffident over control over life. Needs encouragement to achieve potential.

4 Mostly confident; occasional difficulties integrating or in fulfilling social/role activity. Participating in all appropriate decisions. May have difficulty in achieving potential in some situations occasionally.

5 Achieving potential. Autonomous and unrestricted. Able to fulfil social, educational and family role.

WELL-BEING/DISTRESS

0 Severe constant: High and constant levels of distress/upset/concern/frustration/anger/distress/embarrassment/withdrawal/severe depression or apathy, unable to express or control emotions appropriately.

1 Frequently severe: Moderate distress/upset/concern/frustration/anger/distress/embarrassment/withdrawal/severe depression or apathy. Becomes concerned easily, requires constant reassurance/support, needs clear/tight limits and structure, loses emotional control easily.

2 Moderate consistent: Distress/upset/concern/frustration/anger/distress/embarrassment/withdrawal/severe depression or apathy in unfamiliar situations, frequent emotional encouragement and support required.

3 Moderate frequent: Distress/upset/concern/frustration/anger/distress/embarrassment/withdrawal/severe depression or apathy. Controls emotions with assistance, emotionally dependent on some occasions, vulnerable to change in routine, etc., spontaneously uses methods to assist emotional control.

4 Mild occasional: Distress/upset/concern/frustration/anger/distress/embarrassment/withdrawal/severe depression or apathy. Able to control feelings in most situations, generally well adjusted/stable (most of the time/most situations), occasional emotional support/encouragement needed.

5 Not inappropriate: Distress/upset/concern/frustration/anger/distress/embarrassment/withdrawal/severe depression or apathy. Well adjusted, stable and able to cope emotionally with most situations, good insight, accepts and understands own limitations.

7. DYSPHONIA

Identify descriptor that is "best fit". The patient/client does not have to have each feature mentioned. Use 0.5 to indicate if patient/client is slightly better or worse than a descriptor and as appropriate to age.

IMPAIRMENT

0 **Severe persistent aphonia:** Unable or does not phonate.

1 **Consistent dysphonia:** Occasional phonation. May be dysphonic with aphonic episodes.

2 **Moderate dysphonia:** Can phonate but frequent episodes of marked vocal impairment.

3 **Moderate/mild dysphonia:** Less frequent episodes of dysphonia, for example occurs some time each day/or slight persistent "huskiness".

4 **Mild dysphonia:** Occasional episodes of dysphonia occurring, for example on a weekly basis or less.

5 **No dysphonia:** Appropriate/modal voice consistently used.

ACTIVITY

0 Voice production is completely ineffective/inappropriate in all situations.

1 Voice production is completely ineffective/inappropriate in most situations except occasionally with familiar listeners or modified environments.

2 Voice production is effective/appropriate in modified environments, for example quiet situations, familiar situations.

3 Voice production is effective/appropriate but can be unpredictable in some situations. Voice production requires less personal attention and effort in most situations.

4 Voice production is effective/appropriate on most occasions. Rarely effortful. Very occasional difficulties experienced.

5 Voice production is spontaneously effective and appropriate.

PARTICIPATION

0 Unable to fulfil any social/educational/family role. Not involved in decision-making/no autonomy/no control over environment; no social integration.

1 Low self-confidence/poor self-esteem/limited social integration/socially isolated/contributes to some basic and limited decisions. Cannot achieve potential in any situation.

2 Some self-confidence/some social integration/makes some decisions and influences control in familiar situations.

3 Some self-confidence; autonomy emerging. Makes decisions and has control of some aspects of life. Able to achieve some limited social integration/educational activities. Diffident over control over life. Needs encouragement to achieve potential.

4 Mostly confident; occasional difficulties integrating or in fulfilling social/role activity. Participating in all appropriate decisions. May have difficulty in achieving potential in some situations occasionally.

5 Achieving potential. Autonomous and unrestricted. Able to fulfil social, educational and family role.

WELL-BEING/DISTRESS

0 Severe constant: High and constant levels of distress/upset/concern/frustration/anger/distress/embarrassment/withdrawal/severe depression or apathy, unable to express or control emotions appropriately.

1 Frequently severe: Moderate distress/upset/concern/frustration/anger/distress/embarrassment/withdrawal/severe depression or apathy. Becomes concerned easily, requires constant reassurance/support, needs clear/tight limits and structure, loses emotional control easily.

2 Moderate consistent: Distress/upset/concern/frustration/anger/distress/embarrassment/withdrawal/severe depression or apathy in unfamiliar situations, frequent emotional encouragement and support required.

3 Moderate frequent: Distress/upset/concern/frustration/anger/distress/embarrassment/withdrawal/severe depression or apathy. Controls emotions with assistance, emotionally dependent on some occasions, vulnerable to change in routine, etc., spontaneously uses methods to assist emotional control.

4 Mild occasional: Distress/upset/concern/frustration/anger/distress/embarrassment/withdrawal/severe depression or apathy. Able to control feelings in most situations, generally well adjusted/stable (most of the time/most situations), occasional emotional support/encouragement needed.

5 Not inappropriate: Distress/upset/concern/frustration/anger/distress/embarrassment/withdrawal/severe depression or apathy. Well adjusted, stable and able to cope emotionally with most situations, good insight, accepts and understands own limitations.

8. HEARING THERAPY/AURAL REHABILITATION

Identify descriptor that is "best fit". The patient/client does not have to have each feature mentioned. Use 0.5 to indicate if patient/client is slightly better or worse than a descriptor and as appropriate to age.

IMPAIRMENT

0 **Total/profound hearing loss:** Unable to hear any speech or environmental sounds.

1 **Severe hearing loss:** Can perceive very restricted range of environmental and speech sounds.

2 **Severe/moderate hearing loss:** Requires attention to perceive a limited range of speech and environmental sounds.

3 **Moderate hearing loss:** Can hear a range of speech and environmental sounds.

4 **Mild hearing loss:** Unable to hear some specific frequencies; can hear most speech and environmental sounds.

5 **Normal hearing.**

ACTIVITY

0 No functional communication.

1 Limited functional communication with familiar persons or trained persons in familiar and/or adapted environments. Minimal communication with maximal assistance.

2 Limited functional communication. Able to understand 50% speech only from familiar people in known or acoustically favourable environments. Signed support may be of some help, as may amplification and environment aids.

3 Consistent level of general functional communication with familiar and trained persons. Occasional misinterpretation and difficulty with strange or unexpected contexts. Amplification and environmental aids helpful.

4 Able to communicate effectively despite communication irregularities in most situations but may require occasional change in speed or repetition.

5 Consistent effective communication.

PARTICIPATION

0 Unable to fulfil any social/educational/family role. Not involved in decision-making/no autonomy/no control over environment; no social integration.

1 Low self-confidence/poor self-esteem/limited social integration/socially isolated/contributes to some basic and limited decisions. Cannot achieve potential in any situation.

2 Some self-confidence/some social integration/makes some decisions and influences control in familiar situations.

3 Some self-confidence; autonomy emerging. Makes decisions and has control of some aspects of life. Able to achieve some limited social integration/educational activities. Diffident over control over life. Needs encouragement to achieve potential.

4 Mostly confident; occasional difficulties integrating or in fulfilling social/role activity. Participating in all appropriate decisions. May have difficulty in achieving potential in some situations occasionally.

5 Achieving potential. Autonomous and unrestricted. Able to fulfil social, educational and family role.

WELL-BEING/DISTRESS

0 **Severe constant:** High and constant levels of distress/upset/concern/frustration/anger/distress/-embarrassment/withdrawal/severe depression or apathy, unable to express or control emotions appropriately.

1 **Frequently severe:** Moderate distress/upset/concern/frustration/anger/distress/embarrassment/withdrawal/severe depression or apathy. Becomes concerned easily, requires constant reassurance/support, needs clear/tight limits and structure, loses emotional control easily.

2 **Moderate consistent:** Distress/upset/concern/frustration/anger/distress/embarrassment/withdrawal/severe depression or apathy in unfamiliar situations, frequent emotional encouragement and support required.

3 **Moderate frequent:** Distress/upset/concern/frustration/anger/distress/embarrassment/withdrawal/severe depression or apathy. Controls emotions with assistance, emotionally dependent on some occasions, vulnerable to change in routine, etc., spontaneously uses methods to assist emotional control.

4 **Mild occasional:** Distress/upset/concern/frustration/anger/distress/embarrassment/withdrawal/severe depression or apathy. Able to control feelings in most situations, generally well adjusted/stable (most of the time/most situations), occasional emotional support/encouragement needed.

5 **Not inappropriate:** Distress/upset/concern/frustration/anger/distress/embarrassment/withdrawal/severe depression or apathy. Well adjusted, stable and able to cope emotionally with most situations, good insight, accepts and understands own limitations.

9. LARYNGECTOMY

Identify descriptor that is "best fit". The patient/client does not have to have each feature mentioned. Use 0.5 to indicate if patient/client is slightly better or worse than a descriptor and as appropriate to age.

IMPAIRMENT

0 Laryngectomy complicated by stomach pull or requiring skin grafting or colon transplant.
1 Laryngectomy complicated by poor healing, fistulae.
2 Uncomplicated laryngectomy, well healed.
3 Hemi-laryngectomy, removal of one cord and part of thyroid cartilage.
4 Removal of vocal cord or associated soft tissue only.
5 Normal larynx.

ACTIVITY

0 Pseudo voice production is completely ineffective in all situations.
1 Pseudo voice production is completely ineffective in most situations other than with a trained listener or in a modified environment.
2 Pseudo voice production is effective with attention of listener in modified environments, for example quiet situations, familiar situations. Requires considerable effort.
3 Pseudo voice is effective on certain occasions. Pseudo voice requires some personal effort all the time.
4 Pseudo voice is effective on most occasions. Slightly effortful. Able to use the telephone.
5 Pseudo voice is effective in all situations.

PARTICIPATION

0 Unable to fulfil any social/educational/family role. Not involved in decision-making/no autonomy/no control over environment; no social integration.

1 Low self-confidence/poor self-esteem/limited social integration/socially isolated/contributes to some basic and limited decisions. Cannot achieve potential in any situation.

2 Some self-confidence/some social integration/makes some decisions and influences control in familiar situations.

3 Some self-confidence; autonomy emerging. Makes decisions and has control of some aspects of life. Able to achieve some limited social integration/educational activities. Diffident over control over life. Needs encouragement to achieve potential.

4 Mostly confident; occasional difficulties integrating or in fulfilling social/role activity. Participating in all appropriate decisions. May have difficulty in achieving potential in some situations occasionally.

5 Achieving potential. Autonomous and unrestricted. Able to fulfil social, educational and family role.

WELL-BEING/DISTRESS

0 **Severe constant:** High and constant levels of distress/upset/concern/frustration/anger/distress/embarrassment/withdrawal/severe depression or apathy, unable to express or control emotions appropriately.

1 **Frequently severe:** Moderate distress/upset/concern/frustration/anger/distress/embarrassment/withdrawal/severe depression or apathy. Becomes concerned easily, requires constant reassurance/support, needs clear/tight limits and structure, loses emotional control easily.

2 **Moderate consistent:** Distress/upset/concern/frustration/anger/distress/embarrassment/withdrawal/severe depression or apathy in unfamiliar situations, frequent emotional encouragement and support required.

3 **Moderate frequent:** Distress/upset/concern/frustration/anger/distress/embarrassment/withdrawal/severe depression or apathy. Controls emotions with assistance, emotionally dependent on some occasions, vulnerable to change in routine, etc., spontaneously uses methods to assist emotional control.

4 **Mild occasional:** Distress/upset/concern/frustration/anger/distress/embarrassment/withdrawal/severe depression or apathy. Able to control feelings in most situations, generally well adjusted/stable (most of the time/most situations), occasional emotional support/encouragement needed.

5 **Not inappropriate:** Distress/upset/concern/frustration/anger/distress/embarrassment/withdrawal/severe depression or apathy. Well adjusted, stable and able to cope emotionally with most situations, good insight, accepts and understands own limitations.

10. LEARNING DISABILITY – COMMUNICATION

Identify descriptor that is "best fit". The patient/client/client does not have to have each feature mentioned. Use 0.5 to indicate if patient/client is slightly better or worse than a descriptor and as appropriate to age.

IMPAIRMENT

0 **Severe communication impairment:** Multiple areas of impairment including speech/language, sensory and cognition. No communicative intent

1 **Severe/moderate communication impairment:** Several areas of impairment: speech/language, sensory, cognition. May have some slight ability in one area, for example basic recognition.

2 **Moderate communication impairment:** Several areas of moderate impairment: speech/language, sensory, cognitive. There may be one severe overriding difficulty, for example severe articulatory disorder.

3 **Moderate/slight communication impairment:** One moderate impairment with speech/language/ sensory or cognitive. Two or less areas of impairment.

4 **Slight communication impairment:** Slight difficulty with speech/language or sensory; cognitive areas of impairment.

5 **No communication impairment.**

ACTIVITY

0 Unable to communicate in any way. No effective understanding even in context.

1 Shows intentional communication but this is inconsistent. Occasionally able to make simple basic needs known and able to follow stage one instructions in context; can only do this with a trained communication partner in familiar settings. Minimal communication with maximal assistance.

2 Intentional communication consistent. Limited functional communication. Consistently able to make basic needs known and able to follow simple instructions out of context. Communicates better with a trained listener and family members but can occasionally communicate basic needs with unknown people in familiar settings. Depends heavily on context and cues.

3 Consistently able to make basic needs known but can occasionally convey more information than this. Able to follow most everyday simple conversations in context; can communicate just as well with familiar people or strangers in some unfamiliar as well as familiar settings. Needs fewer cues and assistance.

4 Consistently able to convey information but has some difficulty conveying more abstract and complex thoughts. Able to understand almost all everyday conversation but still has occasional difficulty with very complex information. Less context dependent.

5 Communicates well in all situations.

PARTICIPATION

0 Unable to fulfil any social/educational/family role. Not involved in decision-making/no autonomy/no control over environment; no social integration.

1 Low self-confidence/poor self-esteem/limited social integration/socially isolated/contributes to some basic and limited decisions. Cannot achieve potential in any situation.

2 Some self-confidence/some social integration/makes some decisions and influences control in familiar situations.

3 Some self-confidence; autonomy emerging. Makes decisions and has control of some aspects of life. Able to achieve some limited social integration/educational activities. Diffident over control over life. Needs encouragement to achieve potential.

4 Mostly confident; occasional difficulties integrating or in fulfilling social/role activity. Participating in all appropriate decisions. May have difficulty in achieving potential in some situations occasionally.

5 Achieving potential. Autonomous and unrestricted. Able to fulfil social, educational and family role.

WELL-BEING/DISTRESS

0 **Severe constant:** High and constant levels of distress/upset/concern/frustration/anger/distress/embarrassment/withdrawal/severe depression or apathy, unable to express or control emotions appropriately.

1 **Frequently severe:** Moderate distress/upset/concern/frustration/anger/distress/embarrassment/withdrawal/severe depression or apathy. Becomes concerned easily, requires constant reassurance/support, needs clear/tight limits and structure, loses emotional control easily.

2 **Moderate consistent:** Distress/upset/concern/frustration/anger/distress/embarrassment/withdrawal/severe depression or apathy in unfamiliar situations, frequent emotional encouragement and support required.

3 **Moderate frequent:** Distress/upset/concern/frustration/anger/distress/embarrassment/withdrawal/severe depression or apathy. Controls emotions with assistance, emotionally dependent on some occasions, vulnerable to change in routine, etc., spontaneously uses methods to assist emotional control.

4 **Mild occasional:** Distress/upset/concern/frustration/anger/distress/embarrassment/withdrawal/severe depression or apathy. Able to control feelings in most situations, generally well adjusted/stable (most of the time/most situations), occasional emotional support/encouragement needed.

5 **Not inappropriate:** Distress/upset/concern/frustration/anger/distress/embarrassment/withdrawal/severe depression or apathy. Well adjusted, stable and able to cope emotionally with most situations, good insight, accepts and understands own limitations.

11. DYSPRAXIA – CHILDREN WITH DEVELOPMENTAL CO-ORDINATION DIFFICULTIES

Identify descriptor that is "best fit". The patient/client does not have to have each feature mentioned. Use 0.5 to indicate if patient/client is slightly better or worse than a descriptor and as appropriate to age.

IMPAIRMENT

0 Profound problems evident in all areas of sensory-motor development including vestibular, sensory processing and modulation, movement and task planning and organisation, balance and co-ordination. Severe perceptual and ideational difficulties. Severe generalised/motor impairment. Very limited attention to tasks.

1 Severe problems usually involving all areas as indicated above, or may involve severe problems in two or more areas or one profound overriding problem, for example, severe sensory defensiveness or motor impairment.

2 Severe/moderate impairment. Severe to moderate problems in some areas, may involve one severe overriding area, for example gross or fine motor skills, perception, co-ordination, handwriting or movement planning.

3 Moderate impairment. Moderate problems in some areas and/or specific moderate problems in one area, such as motor skills, organisation, concentration, writing or perception.

4 Mild impairment. Mild problems in one or more areas involving fine or gross motor skills, perception, co-ordination, attention, praxis.

5 Age-appropriate motor and perceptual development in all areas.

ACTIVITY

0 Unable to function independently in any way. Unable to perform any activity without skilled and continual assistance, specialised equipment, supervision or simplification.

1 Occasionally able to perform some simple/automatic activities independently, or to perform some small parts of some tasks alone. Minimal function with maximum assistance.

2 Able to perform basic simple tasks or parts of more complex tasks. Works better with a familiar adult or family member, but lacks confidence or ability in unfamiliar situations. Difficulty learning new skills or transferring them to different situations. Verbal prompts help.

3 Consistently able to perform simple tasks or parts of more complex ones without help. Can occasionally attempt new tasks building on existing skills. Needs help for some activities, or extra time, or tasks to be broken down or simplified. Verbal prompting may be needed.

4 Occasional difficulties experienced in certain situations or with certain activities. May require extra time to complete tasks. Occasional verbal prompts.

5 Functions well in all situations and is fully independent at an age-appropriate level.

PARTICIPATION

0 Unable to fulfil any social/educational/family role. Not involved in decision-making/no autonomy/no control over environment, no social integration.

1 Low self-confidence/poor self-esteem/limited social integration/socially isolated/contributes to some basic and limited decisions. Cannot achieve potential in any situation.

2 Some self-confidence/some social integration/makes some decisions and influences control in familiar situations.

3 Some self-confidence; autonomy emerging. Makes decisions and has control of some aspects of life. Able to achieve some limited social integration/educational activities. Diffident over control over life. Needs encouragement to achieve potential.

4 Mostly confident; occasional difficulties integrating or in fulfilling social/role activity. Participating in all appropriate decisions. May have difficulty in achieving potential in some situations occasionally.

5 Achieving potential. Autonomous and unrestricted. Able to fulfil social, educational and family role.

WELL-BEING/DISTRESS

0 **Severe constant:** High and constant levels of distress/upset/concern/frustration/anger/distress/embarrassment/withdrawal/severe depression or apathy, unable to express or control emotions appropriately.

1 **Frequently severe:** Moderate distress/upset/concern/frustration/anger/distress/embarrassment/withdrawal/severe depression or apathy. Becomes concerned easily, requires constant reassurance/support, needs clear/tight limits and structure, loses emotional control easily.

2 **Moderate consistent:** Distress/upset/concern/frustration/anger/distress/embarrassment/withdrawal/severe depression or apathy in unfamiliar situations, frequent emotional encouragement and support required.

3 **Moderate frequent:** Distress/upset/concern/frustration/anger/distress/embarrassment/withdrawal/severe depression or apathy. Controls emotions with assistance, emotionally dependent on some occasions, vulnerable to change in routine, etc., spontaneously uses methods to assist emotional control.

4 **Mild occasional:** Distress/upset/concern/frustration/anger/distress/embarrassment/withdrawal/severe depression or apathy. Able to control feelings in most situations, generally well adjusted/stable (most of the time/most situations), occasional emotional support/encouragement needed.

5 **Not inappropriate:** Distress/upset/concern/frustration/anger/distress/embarrassment/withdrawal/severe depression or apathy. Well adjusted, stable and able to cope emotionally with most situations, good insight, accepts and understands own limitations.

12. CEREBRAL PALSY

Identify descriptor that is "best fit". The patient/client does not have to have each feature mentioned. Use 0.5 to indicate if patient/client is slightly better or worse than a descriptor and as appropriate to age.

IMPAIRMENT

0 Severe abnormality of tone with total body involvement. Fixed or at risk of severe contractures and deformities. No voluntary movement. Severe sensory impairment.

1 Severe abnormality of tone with total body involvement. At risk of severe contractures and deformities. Minimal voluntary movement. Severe sensory impairment.

2 Moderate abnormality of tone with total body involvement or severe involvement of 2 limbs. At risk of contractures and deformities. Potential for voluntary movement. Moderate sensory impairment.

3 Moderate abnormality of tone with partial involvement or severe single limb involvement. Little risk of contractures or deformities. Impaired voluntary movement. Mild sensory impairment.

4 Mild abnormality of tone with no contractures and deformities. Mild impairment in voluntary movement. Minimal sensory impairment.

5 No impairment.

ACTIVITY

0 No purposeful active movement, totally dependent, requires full physical care and constant vigilant supervision. May have totally disruptive and uncooperative behaviour. Totally dependant on skilled assistance.

1 Some very limited purposeful activity. Bed/chair bound but unable to sit independently. Needs high level of assistance in most tasks. Some awareness, some effort and recognition to contribute to care. Dependent on skilled assistance.

2 Participating in care and engaging in some structured activity. Limited self-help skills. Initiates some aspects of activities of daily living (ADL). Transfers with one, mobilises with two. Requires physical and verbal prompting and supervision for most tasks and movements Dependent on familiar assistant.

3 Appropriately initiating activities. Transfers or walking requires supervision or help of one. Undertakes personal care in modified supported environment. Needs assistance or supervision with some unfamiliar or complex tasks.

4 Carrying out personal care and tasks but is less efficient, requires extra time, or may need encouragement, uses prompts effectively. Minimal or occasional assistance required for some complex tasks.

5 Age-appropriate independence.

PARTICIPATION

0 Unable to fulfil any social/educational/family role. Not involved in decision-making/no autonomy/no control over environment; no social integration.

1 Low self-confidence/poor self-esteem/limited social integration/socially isolated/contributes to some basic and limited decisions. Cannot achieve potential in any situation.

2 Some self-confidence/some social integration/makes some decisions and influences control in familiar situations.

3 Some self-confidence; autonomy emerging. Makes decisions and has control of some aspects of life. Able to achieve some limited social integration/educational activities. Diffident over control over life. Needs encouragement to achieve potential.

4 Mostly confident; occasional difficulties integrating or in fulfilling social/role activity. Participating in all appropriate decisions. May have difficulty in achieving potential in some situations occasionally.

5 Achieving potential. Autonomous and unrestricted. Able to fulfil social, educational and family role.

WELL-BEING/DISTRESS

0 **Severe constant:** High and constant levels of distress/upset/concern/frustration/anger/distress/embarrassment/withdrawal/severe depression or apathy, unable to express or control emotions appropriately.

1 **Frequently severe:** Moderate distress/upset/concern/frustration/anger/distress/embarrassment/withdrawal/severe depression or apathy. Becomes concerned easily, requires constant reassurance/support, needs clear/tight limits and structure, loses emotional control easily.

2 **Moderate consistent:** Distress/upset/concern/frustration/anger/distress/embarrassment/withdrawal/severe depression or apathy in unfamiliar situations, frequent emotional encouragement and support required.

3 **Moderate frequent:** Distress/upset/concern/frustration/anger/distress/embarrassment/withdrawal/severe depression or apathy. Controls emotions with assistance, emotionally dependent on some occasions, vulnerable to change in routine, etc., spontaneously uses methods to assist emotional control.

4 **Mild occasional:** Distress/upset/concern/frustration/anger/distress/embarrassment/withdrawal/severe depression or apathy. Able to control feelings in most situations, generally well adjusted/stable (most of the time/most situations), occasional emotional support/encouragement needed.

5 **Not inappropriate:** Distress/upset/concern/frustration/anger/distress/embarrassment/withdrawal/severe depression or apathy. Well adjusted, stable and able to cope emotionally with most situations, good insight, accepts and understands own limitations.

13. COGNITION

Identify descriptor that is "best fit". The patient/client does not have to have each feature mentioned. Use 0.5 to indicate if patient/client is slightly better or worse than a descriptor and as appropriate to age.

IMPAIRMENT

0 Unresponsive to all stimuli. Does not recognise people, unable to learn, poor memory responses.

1 Non-purposeful random or fragmented responses. Occasionally responds to some simple commands; may respond to discomfort; responses may be severely delayed or inappropriate. Recognises familiar people and routine tasks in context. Cooperates occasionally, attempts to learn simplest routines with maximal assistance.

2 Inconsistent reaction directly related to type of stimulus presented. Occasionally responds appropriately. Can attend but is highly distractible and unable to focus on a particular task. Memory is severely impaired; may perform previously learned task with structure.

3 Recognises familiar people and tasks in most contexts, able to retain small amounts of information consistently. Responds appropriately with some consistency, appears oriented to setting, but insight, judgement and problem solving poor. Memory variable – sometimes good able to learn more complex task.

4 Alert and able to learn but needs occasional prompts and assistance, responds well in most situations. Able to recall and integrate past and recent events; shows carryover for new learning and needs no supervision when activities are learned, but has high-level difficulties for example, abstract reasoning, tolerance for stress, or judgement in unusual circumstances.

5 No cognitive impairment. responds appropriately is alert and able to learn,

ACTIVITY

0 Inability to recognise body functions and requirements. May have totally disruptive and uncooperative behaviour. Totally dependent requires full physical care and constant vigilant supervision.

1 Recognises bodily requirements and occasionally initiates activity but requires a high level of assistance in most tasks.

2 Able to self care and relate to others in protected environment but is dependent on constant verbal prompting and direction.

3 Needs occasional verbal prompting to initiate activity. Able to operate without supervision for short periods, able to have some independence with encouragement, independent in familiar surroundings only.

4 Able to live independently with some occasional support, requires extra time, encouragement. Assistance required with unfamiliar tasks.

5 Age-appropriate independence.

PARTICIPATION

0 Unable to fulfil any social/educational/family role. Not involved in decision-making/no autonomy/no control over environment; no social integration.

1 Low self-confidence/poor self-esteem/limited social integration/socially isolated/contributes to some basic and limited decisions. Cannot achieve potential in any situation.

2 Some self-confidence/some social integration/makes some decisions and influences control in familiar situations.

3 Some self-confidence; autonomy emerging. Makes decisions and has control of some aspects of life. Able to achieve some limited social integration/educational activities. Diffident over control over life. Needs encouragement to achieve potential.

4 Mostly confident; occasional difficulties integrating or in fulfilling social/role activity. Participating in all appropriate decisions. May have difficulty in achieving potential in some situations occasionally.

5 Achieving potential. Autonomous and unrestricted. Able to fulfil social, educational and family role.

WELL-BEING/DISTRESS

0 **Severe constant:** High and constant levels of distress/upset/concern/frustration/anger/distress/embarrassment/withdrawal/severe depression or apathy, unable to express or control emotions appropriately.

1 **Frequently severe:** Moderate distress/upset/concern/frustration/anger/distress/embarrassment/withdrawal/severe depression or apathy. Becomes concerned easily, requires constant reassurance/support, needs clear/tight limits and structure, loses emotional control easily.

2 **Moderate consistent:** Distress/upset/concern/frustration/anger/distress/embarrassment/withdrawal/severe depression or apathy in unfamiliar situations, frequent emotional encouragement and support required.

3 **Moderate frequent:** Distress/upset/concern/frustration/anger/distress/embarrassment/withdrawal/severe depression or apathy. Controls emotions with assistance, emotionally dependent on some occasions, vulnerable to change in routine, etc., spontaneously uses methods to assist emotional control.

4 **Mild occasional:** Distress/upset/concern/frustration/anger/distress/embarrassment/withdrawal/severe depression or apathy. Able to control feelings in most situations, generally well adjusted/stable (most of the time/most situations), occasional emotional support/encouragement needed.

5 **Not inappropriate:** Distress/upset/concern/frustration/anger/distress/embarrassment/withdrawal/severe depression or apathy. Well adjusted, stable and able to cope emotionally with most situations, good insight, accepts and understands own limitations.

14. HEAD INJURY

Identify descriptor that is "best fit". The patient/client does not have to have each feature mentioned. Use 0.5 to indicate if patient/client is slightly better or worse than a descriptor and as appropriate to age.

IMPAIRMENT

0 Inability to respond to external stimuli/gross loss of passive range of movement affecting multiple joints. Debilitated, minimal muscle power, multi-joint contractures/swelling. Total flaccidity/severe spasticity. Severe continual involuntary movements. Total loss of righting and equilibrium reactions. Severe global symptoms.

1 Responsive but uncooperative, range of movement maximally restricted. Passive range of movement moderately restricted. Pain on passive movement. No standing balance. Unable to weight bear. Minimal controlled voluntary movement. Severe sensory inattention. Low tone/moderate spasticity. Strong associated reactions. Severe degree of several signs and symptoms, for example, dense hemiplegia poor trunk control and some perceptual deficit.

2 Range of movement moderately restricted. Pain on active movement. Poor static balance. Some controlled purposeful movement. Moderate to severe inattention. Moderate involuntary movement. Associated reactions occurring on preparation to movement.

3 Some active participation, active range of movement with minimal restriction. Some associated reactions during movement. Purposeful but not necessarily accurate voluntary movement. Moderate sensory inattention. Minimal involuntary movement. Intermittent pain on active movement. Poor dynamic standing balance. May have one severe sign or symptom alone, for example, dense hemiplegia or severe perceptual deficit or combination of milder signs or symptoms, for example, mild hemiparesis with some sensory loss and occasional incontinence.

4 Slight/minimal abnormality of strength, muscle tone, range of movement. Difficulty with balance, purposeful accurate voluntary movements. May have abnormal speed of movement, slight incoordination. Minimal associated reaction with efforts.

5 Age-appropriate strength, range of movement and co-ordination. Normal tone and active movements.

ACTIVITY

0 No purposeful active movement, totally dependent, requires full physical care and constant vigilant supervision. May have totally disruptive and uncooperative behaviour. Dependent on skilled assistance.

1 Bed/chair bound but unable to sit independently. Some very limited purposeful activity. Needs high level of assistance in most tasks. Some awareness, some effort and recognition to contribute to care. Dependent on skilled assistance.

2 Head and trunk control. Limited self-help skills. Initiates some aspects of ADL. Transfers with one, mobilises with 2. Requires physical and verbal prompting and supervision for most tasks and movements. Participating in care and engaging in some structured activity. Dependent on familiar assistant.

3 Transfers or walking requires supervision or help of one. Undertakes personal care in modified supported environment. Appropriately initiating activities and needs assistance or supervision with some unfamiliar or complex tasks. Initiates activities appropriately.

4 Carrying out personal care and tasks but is less efficient (clumsy), requires extra time or may need encouragement, assistance with unfamiliar tasks. Minimal or occasional assistance required for some complex tasks.

5 Age-appropriate independence.

PARTICIPATION

0 Unable to fulfil any social/educational/family role. Not involved in decision-making/no autonomy/no control over environment; no social integration.

1 Low self-confidence/poor self-esteem/limited social integration/socially isolated/contributes to some basic and limited decisions. Cannot achieve potential in any situation.

2 Some self-confidence/some social integration/makes some decisions and influences control in familiar situations.

3 Some self-confidence; autonomy emerging. Makes decisions and has control of some aspects of life. Able to achieve some limited social integration/educational activities. Diffident over control over life. Needs encouragement to achieve potential.

4 Mostly confident; occasional difficulties integrating or in fulfilling social/role activity. Participating in all appropriate decisions. May have difficulty in achieving potential in some situations occasionally.

5 Achieving potential. Autonomous and unrestricted. Able to fulfil social, educational and family role.

WELL-BEING/DISTRESS

0 **Severe constant:** High and constant levels of distress/upset/concern/frustration/anger/distress/embarrassment/withdrawal/severe depression or apathy, unable to express or control emotions appropriately.

1 **Frequently severe:** Moderate distress/upset/concern/frustration/anger/distress/embarrassment/withdrawal/severe depression or apathy. Becomes concerned easily, requires constant reassurance/support, needs clear/tight limits and structure, loses emotional control easily.

2 **Moderate consistent:** Distress/upset/concern/frustration/anger/distress/embarrassment/withdrawal/severe depression or apathy in unfamiliar situations, frequent emotional encouragement and support required.

3 **Moderate frequent:** Distress/upset/concern/frustration/anger/distress/embarrassment/withdrawal/severe depression or apathy. Controls emotions with assistance, emotionally dependent on some occasions, vulnerable to change in routine, etc., spontaneously uses methods to assist emotional control.

4 **Mild occasional:** Distress/upset/concern/frustration/anger/distress/embarrassment/withdrawal/severe depression or apathy. Able to control feelings in most situations, generally well adjusted/stable (most of the time/most situations), occasional emotional support/encouragement needed.

5 **Not inappropriate:** Distress/upset/concern/frustration/anger/distress/embarrassment/withdrawal/severe depression or apathy. Well adjusted, stable and able to cope emotionally with most situations, good insight, accepts and understands own limitations.

15. STROKE

Identify descriptor that is "best fit". The patient/client does not have to have each feature mentioned. Use 0.5 to indicate if patient/client is slightly better or worse than a descriptor and as appropriate to age.

IMPAIRMENT

0 No voluntary movement, severe flaccidity or spasticity, gross sensory impairment, may have a loss of bowel and bladder control. Unresponsive.

1 Severe degree of several signs and symptoms, for example, dense hemiplegia, severe perceptual deficit, occasional control of bladder and bowel, severe cognitive deficit, strong associated reactions with very limited range of passive movements. Responsive.

2 Moderate degree of several signs and symptoms, for example, moderate hemiplegia and some dyspraxia, may have some bowel/bladder dysfunction. Active movement with gravity eliminated, control patterns of movement, moderate associated reactions, severe to moderate sensory deficit.

3 Active movement against gravity, controlled isolated movement, occasional associated reactions, moderate sensory inattention, movements may not be accurate, or one severe sign/symptom, for example, dense hemiplegic arm, or two moderate signs/symptoms, for example, moderate arm/leg hemiplegia.

4 Loss of fine active movement and co-ordination, minimal sensory deficit, loss of end range of movement. Slight incoordination or loss of power in limb/s, occasional perceptual cognitive or perceptual difficulties.

5 No impairment.

ACTIVITY

0 No purposeful active movement, totally dependent, requires full physical care and constant vigilant supervision. May have totally disruptive and uncooperative behaviour. Dependent on skilled assistance.

1 Bed/chair bound but unable to sit independently. Some very limited purposeful activity. Needs high level of assistance in most tasks. Some awareness, some effort and recognition to contribute to care. Dependent on skilled assistance.

2 Head and trunk control. Limited self-help skills. Initiates some aspects of ADL. Transfers with one, mobilises with two. Requires physical and verbal prompting and supervision for most tasks and movements. Participating in care and engaging in some structured activity. Dependent on skilled assistance.

3 Transfers or walking requires supervision or help of one. Undertakes personal care in modified supported environment. Initiates activities appropriately. Appropriately initiating activities and needs assistance or supervision with some unfamiliar or complex tasks.

4 Carrying out personal care and tasks but is less efficient, clumsy, requires extra time or may need encouragement. Uses memory prompts effectively. Minimal or occasional assistance required for some complex tasks.

5 Age-appropriate independence.

PARTICIPATION

0 Unable to fulfil any social/educational/family role. Not involved in decision-making/no autonomy/no control over environment; no social integration.

1 Low self-confidence/poor self-esteem/limited social integration/socially isolated/contributes to some basic and limited decisions. Cannot achieve potential in any situation.

2 Some self-confidence/some social integration/makes some decisions and influences control in familiar situations.

3 Some self-confidence; autonomy emerging. Makes decisions and has control of some aspects of life. Able to achieve some limited social integration/educational activities. Diffident over control over life. Needs encouragement to achieve potential.

4 Mostly confident; occasional difficulties integrating or in fulfilling social/role activity. Participating in all appropriate decisions. May have difficulty in achieving potential in some situations occasionally.

5 Achieving potential. Autonomous and unrestricted. Able to fulfil social, educational and family role.

WELL-BEING/DISTRESS

0 **Severe constant:** High and constant levels of distress/upset/concern/frustration/anger/distress/embarrassment/withdrawal/severe depression or apathy, unable to express or control emotions appropriately.

1 **Frequently severe:** Moderate distress/upset/concern/frustration/anger/distress/embarrassment/withdrawal/severe depression or apathy. Becomes concerned easily, requires constant reassurance/support, needs clear/tight limits and structure, loses emotional control easily.

2 **Moderate consistent:** Distress/upset/concern/frustration/anger/distress/embarrassment/withdrawal/severe depression or apathy in unfamiliar situations, frequent emotional encouragement and support required.

3 **Moderate frequent:** Distress/upset/concern/frustration/anger/distress/embarrassment/withdrawal/severe depression or apathy. Controls emotions with assistance, emotionally dependent on some occasions, vulnerable to change in routine, etc., spontaneously uses methods to assist emotional control.

4 **Mild occasional:** Distress/upset/concern/frustration/anger/distress/embarrassment/withdrawal/severe depression or apathy. Able to control feelings in most situations, generally well adjusted/stable (most of the time/most situations), occasional emotional support/encouragement needed.

5 **Not inappropriate:** Distress/upset/concern/frustration/anger/distress/embarrassment/withdrawal/severe depression or apathy. Well adjusted, stable and able to cope emotionally with most situations, good insight, accepts and understands own limitations.

16. CARDIAC REHABILITATION

Identify descriptor that is "best fit". The patient/client does not have to have each feature mentioned. Use 0.5 to indicate if patient/client is slightly better or worse than a descriptor and as appropriate to age.

IMPAIRMENT

0 Severe uncontrolled angina, uncontrolled cardiac failure.

1 Moderate control of cardiac function with multiple drug therapy.

2 Cardiac function and angina mostly controlled with regular medication, at times not controlled.

3 Cardiac function and angina controlled with regular medication.

4 Cardiac function and angina controlled with occasional or minimal medication.

5 Normal cardiac function.

ACTIVITY

0 Lacks functional ability, dependent due to severe chest pain/breathlessness/weakness/dizziness on minimal exertion – i.e. when being transferred bed to chair (room bound).

1 Very limited functional ability, chest pain/breathlessness/weakness/dizziness limiting activities of daily living, i.e. washing, dressing, mobilising to toilet (house bound).

2 Function limited by chest pain/breathlessness/weakness/dizziness, for example, walking on level ground (50 yards) or one flight of stairs (house/immediate environment bound).

3 Moderate functional ability, chest pain/breathlessness/weakness/dizziness on moderate exertion, i.e. one minute each stage of 10 stage exercise circuit (local environment).

4 Mild affect on functional ability, some occasional reduction in complex or demanding tasks due to pain/breathlessness.

5 No functional disability – able to tackle normal activities.

PARTICIPATION

0 Unable to fulfil any social/educational/family role. Not involved in decision-making/no autonomy/no control over environment; no social integration.

1 Low self-confidence/poor self-esteem/limited social integration/socially isolated/contributes to some basic and limited decisions. Cannot achieve potential in any situation.

2 Some self-confidence/some social integration/makes some decisions and influences control in familiar situations.

3 Some self-confidence; autonomy emerging. Makes decisions and has control of some aspects of life. Able to achieve some limited social integration/educational activities. Diffident over control over life. Needs encouragement to achieve potential.

4 Mostly confident; occasional difficulties integrating or in fulfilling social/role activity. Participating in all appropriate decisions. May have difficulty in achieving potential in some situations occasionally.

5 Achieving potential. Autonomous and unrestricted. Able to fulfil social, educational and family role.

WELL-BEING/DISTRESS

0 **Severe constant:** High and constant levels of distress/upset/concern/frustration/anger/distress/embarrassment/withdrawal/severe depression or apathy, unable to express or control emotions appropriately.

1 **Frequently severe:** Moderate distress/upset/concern/frustration/anger/distress/embarrassment/withdrawal/severe depression or apathy. Becomes concerned easily, requires constant reassurance/support, needs clear/tight limits and structure, loses emotional control easily.

2 **Moderate consistent:** Distress/upset/concern/frustration/anger/distress/embarrassment/withdrawal/severe depression or apathy in unfamiliar situations, frequent emotional encouragement and support required.

3 **Moderate frequent:** Distress/upset/concern/frustration/anger/distress/embarrassment/withdrawal/severe depression or apathy. Controls emotions with assistance, emotionally dependent on some occasions, vulnerable to change in routine, etc., spontaneously uses methods to assist emotional control.

4 **Mild occasional:** Distress/upset/concern/frustration/anger/distress/embarrassment/withdrawal/severe depression or apathy. Able to control feelings in most situations, generally well adjusted/stable (most of the time/most situations), occasional emotional support/encouragement needed.

5 **Not inappropriate:** Distress/upset/concern/frustration/anger/distress/embarrassment/withdrawal/severe depression or apathy. Well adjusted, stable and able to cope emotionally with most situations, good insight, accepts and understands own limitations.

17. NEUROLOGICAL DISORDERS (INCLUDING PROGRESSIVE NEUROLOGICAL DISORDERS)

Identify descriptor that is "best fit". The patient/client does not have to have each feature mentioned. Use 0.5 to indicate if patient/client is slightly better or worse than a descriptor and as appropriate to age.

IMPAIRMENT

0 No volitional movement. Total flaccidity/severe spasticity. Total sensory inattention. Severe continual involuntary movement. Total loss of righting plus equilibrium reactions. Severe global symptoms. May be primarily bed bound.
1 Occasional minimal voluntary movements. Severe loss of motor or sensory function, with severe flaccidity/spasticity. All limbs and trunk affected. Moderate to severe involuntary movements. Severe sensory inattention.
2 Frequent voluntary movements. Moderate involuntary movement. General associated reactions occurring on preparation to movement. Moderate to severe inattention.
3 Minimal involuntary movements. Severe abnormal tone in specific muscle groups or moderate impairment of tone globally. Specific associated reactions during preparation to move. Purposeful and controlled but not necessarily accurate or strong voluntary movement. Moderate sensory inattention.
4 Mild abnormality of tone or minimal or occasional associated reactions with effort. Can control tone but occasional abnormal tone, for example, after activity. Purposeful accurate voluntary movement. Abnormal speed of movement. Minimal sensory inattention.
5 Normal purposeful skilled movement. Normal tone, normal sensory awareness, normal righting and equilibrium reactions, alert and orientated.

ACTIVITY

0 No purposeful active movement, totally dependent, requires full physical care and constant vigilant supervision. May have totally disruptive and uncooperative behaviour. Dependent on skilled assistance.
1 Bed/chair bound but unable to sit independently. Transfers with maximal assistance, wheel-chair dependent, unable to stand unsupported. Some very limited purposeful activity. Needs high level of assistance in all tasks. Some awareness, some effort and recognition to contribute to care. Dependent on skilled assistance.
2 Head and trunk control. Limited self-help skills. Initiates some aspects of ADL. Transfers with one, mobilises with two. Requires physical and/or verbal prompting and supervision for most tasks and movements. Participating in care and engaging in some structured activity. Dependent on skilled assistance.
3 Stands unsupported, transfers or walking requires supervision or help of one. "House hold walker". Undertakes personal care in modified supported environment. Appropriately initiating activities and needs assistance or supervision with some unfamiliar or complex tasks. Initiates activities appropriately. Ability varies with time of day.
4 Carrying out personal care and tasks but is less efficient, clumsy, requires extra time or may need encouragement. Uses prompts effectively. Minimal or occasional assistance required for some complex tasks.
5 Age-appropriate independence.

PARTICIPATION

0 Unable to fulfil any social/educational/family role. Not involved in decision-making/no autonomy/no control over environment; no social integration.

1 Low self-confidence/poor self-esteem/limited social integration/socially isolated/contributes to some basic and limited decisions. Cannot achieve potential in any situation.

2 Some self-confidence/some social integration/makes some decisions and influences control in familiar situations.

3 Some self-confidence; autonomy emerging. Makes decisions and has control of some aspects of life. Able to achieve some limited social integration/educational activities. Diffident over control over life. Needs encouragement to achieve potential.

4 Mostly confident; occasional difficulties integrating or in fulfilling social/role activity. Participating in all appropriate decisions. May have difficulty in achieving potential in some situations occasionally.

5 Achieving potential. Autonomous and unrestricted. Able to fulfil social, educational and family role.

WELL-BEING/DISTRESS

0 **Severe constant:** High and constant levels of distress/upset/concern/frustration/anger/distress/embarrassment/withdrawal/severe depression or apathy, unable to express or control emotions appropriately.

1 **Frequently severe:** Moderate distress/upset/concern/frustration/anger/distress/embarrassment/withdrawal/severe depression or apathy. Becomes concerned easily, requires constant reassurance/support, needs clear/tight limits and structure, loses emotional control easily.

2 **Moderate consistent:** Distress/upset/concern/frustration/anger/distress/embarrassment/withdrawal/severe depression or apathy in unfamiliar situations, frequent emotional encouragement and support required.

3 **Moderate frequent:** Distress/upset/concern/frustration/anger/distress/embarrassment/withdrawal/severe depression or apathy. Controls emotions with assistance, emotionally dependent on some occasions, vulnerable to change in routine, etc., spontaneously uses methods to assist emotional control.

4 **Mild occasional:** Distress/upset/concern/frustration/anger/distress/embarrassment/withdrawal/severe depression or apathy. Able to control feelings in most situations, generally well adjusted/stable (most of the time/most situations), occasional emotional support/encouragement needed.

5 **Not inappropriate:** Distress/upset/concern/frustration/anger/distress/embarrassment/withdrawal/severe depression or apathy. Well adjusted, stable and able to cope emotionally with most situations, good insight, accepts and understands own limitations.

18. COMPLEX AND MULTIPLE DIFFICULTY

Identify descriptor that is "best fit". The patient/client does not have to have each feature mentioned. Use 0.5 to indicate if patient/client is slightly better or worse than a descriptor and as appropriate to age.

IMPAIRMENT

0 No active movement, severe abnormality of muscle tone and patterns of movement. May have abnormal sensory loss, severe fixed deformities, severe respiratory difficulties. Presence of pathological reflexes.

1 Grossly abnormal muscle tone, occasionally some voluntary movement towards stimulus, some contractures, some pathological reflexes, sensory impairment, severely restricted range of movement, frequent respiratory difficulties.

2 Altered muscle tone, some controlled purposeful active movement. Some abnormal primitive reflexes. Some joint contractures, may have sensory impairment.

3 Some useful strength, but abnormal muscle tone, coordinates movement but without accuracy, requires large stable base and low centre of gravity, moderate sensory impairment.

4 Slight abnormality of strength, muscle tone, range of movement; minimal involuntary movements. Slightly impaired neurology with mild weakness or incoordination.

5 Age-appropriate tone, strength, range of movement, co-ordination and sensation.

ACTIVITY

0 No purposeful active movement, totally dependent, requires full physical care and constant vigilant supervision. May have totally disruptive and uncooperative behaviour. Dependent on skilled assistance.

1 Bed/chair bound but unable to sit independently. Some very limited purposeful activity. Needs high level of assistance in most tasks. Some awareness, some effort and recognition to contribute to care. Dependent on skilled assistance.

2 Head and trunk control. Limited self-help skills. Initiates some aspects of ADL. Transfers with one, mobilises with two. Requires physical and verbal prompting and supervision for most tasks and movements. Participating in care and engaging in some structured activity. Dependent on familiar assistance.

3 Transfers or walking requires supervision or help of one. Undertakes personal care in modified supported environment. Appropriately initiating activities and needs assistance or supervision with some unfamiliar or complex tasks. Initiates activities appropriately.

4 Carrying out personal care and tasks but is less efficient, requires extra time or may need encouragement. Uses memory prompts or other aids effectively. Minimal or occasional assistance required for some complex or unfamiliar tasks.

5 Age-appropriate independence.

PARTICIPATION

0 Unable to fulfil any social/educational/family role. Not involved in decision-making/no autonomy/no control over environment; no social integration.

1 Low self-confidence/poor self-esteem/limited social integration/socially isolated/contributes to some basic and limited decisions. Cannot achieve potential in any situation.

2 Some self-confidence/some social integration/makes some decisions and influences control in familiar situations.

3 Some self-confidence; autonomy emerging. Makes decisions and has control of some aspects of life. Able to achieve some limited social integration/educational activities. Diffident over control over life. Needs encouragement to achieve potential.

4 Mostly confident; occasional difficulties integrating or in fulfilling social/role activity. Participating in all appropriate decisions. May have difficulty in achieving potential in some situations occasionally.

5 Achieving potential. Autonomous and unrestricted. Able to fulfil social, educational and family role.

WELL-BEING/DISTRESS

0 **Severe constant:** High and constant levels of distress/upset/concern/frustration/anger/distress/embarrassment/withdrawal/severe depression or apathy, unable to express or control emotions appropriately.

1 **Frequently severe:** Moderate distress/upset/concern/frustration/anger/distress/embarrassment/withdrawal/severe depression or apathy. Becomes concerned easily, requires constant reassurance/support, needs clear/tight limits and structure, loses emotional control easily.

2 **Moderate consistent:** Distress/upset/concern/frustration/anger/distress/embarrassment/withdrawal/severe depression or apathy in unfamiliar situations, frequent emotional encouragement and support required.

3 **Moderate frequent:** Distress/upset/concern/frustration/anger/distress/embarrassment/withdrawal/severe depression or apathy. Controls emotions with assistance, emotionally dependent on some occasions, vulnerable to change in routine, etc., spontaneously uses methods to assist emotional control.

4 **Mild occasional:** Distress/upset/concern/frustration/anger/distress/embarrassment/withdrawal/severe depression or apathy. Able to control feelings in most situations, generally well adjusted/stable (most of the time/most situations), occasional emotional support/encouragement needed.

5 **Not inappropriate:** Distress/upset/concern/frustration/anger/distress/embarrassment/withdrawal/severe depression or apathy. Well adjusted, stable and able to cope emotionally with most situations, good insight, accepts and understands own limitations.

19. MULTI-FACTORIAL CONDITIONS

Includes complex physical disability and frail elderly

Identify descriptor that is "best fit". The patient/client does not have to have each feature mentioned. Use 0.5 to indicate if patient/client is slightly better or worse than a descriptor and as appropriate to age.

IMPAIRMENT

0 Inability to respond to external stimuli/gross loss of passive range of movement affecting multiple joints. Debilitated, minimal muscle power, multi-joint contractures/swelling. Total flaccidity/severe spasticity. Severe continual involuntary movements. Total loss of righting and equilibrium reactions. Global severity of all symptoms.

1 Responsive but uncooperative, range of movement maximally restricted, multiple joint involvement. Passive range of movement moderately restricted. Pain on passive movement. No standing balance. Unable to weight bear. Minimal voluntary movement. Severe sensory inattention. Low tone/moderate spasticity. Strong associated reactions. Severe degree of several signs and symptoms, for example, dense hemiplegia with some perceptual deficit. Responsive.

2 Aware and some co-operation. Active range of movement moderately restricted. Contractures in more than one joint. Pain on active movement. Poor static balance. Occasional purposeful movement. Moderate to severe inattention. Moderate involuntary movement. Associated reactions occurring on preparation to movement.

3 Aware and actively co-operative Some active participation, active functional range of movement with minimal restriction. Intermittent pain on active movement. Poor dynamic standing balance, at risk of contractions. Some associated reactions during movement. Purposeful but not necessarily accurate voluntary movement. Moderate sensory inattention. Minimal involuntary movement. May have one severe sign or symptom alone, for example, dense hemiplegia or severe perceptual deficit or combination of milder signs or symptoms, for example, mild hemiparesis with some sensory loss.

4 Co-operative, may have mild occasional inattention. Slight/minimal abnormality of strength, muscle tone, range of movement. Occasional difficulty with balance, purposeful accurate voluntary movements. May have abnormal speed of movement, slight incoordination. Minimal associated reaction with efforts.

5 Age-appropriate strength, range of movement and co-ordination. Normal tone and active movements.

ACTIVITY

0 No purposeful active movement, totally dependent, requires full physical care and constant vigilant supervision. May have totally disruptive and uncooperative behaviour. Dependent on skilled assistance.

1 Bed/chair bound but unable to sit independently. Some very limited purposeful activity. Needs high level of assistance in most tasks. Some awareness, some effort and recognition to contribute to care. Dependent on skilled assistance.

2 Head and trunk control. Limited self-help skills. Initiates some aspects of ADL. Transfers with one, mobilises with two. Requires physical and verbal prompting and supervision for most tasks and movements. Participating in care and engaging in some structured activity. Dependent on skilled assistance.

3 Transfers or walking requires supervision or help of one. Undertakes personal care in modified supported environment. Appropriately initiating activities and needs assistance or supervision with some unfamiliar or complex tasks. Initiates activities appropriately.

4 Carrying out personal care and tasks but is less efficient, clumsy, requires extra time or may need encouragement. Uses memory prompts effectively. Minimal or occasional assistance required for some complex tasks.

5 Age-appropriate independence.

PARTICIPATION

0 Unable to fulfil any social/educational/family role. Not involved in decision-making/no autonomy/no control over environment; no social integration.
1 Low self-confidence/poor self-esteem/limited social integration/socially isolated/contributes to some basic and limited decisions. Cannot achieve potential in any situation.
2 Some self-confidence/some social integration/makes some decisions and influences control in familiar situations.
3 Some self-confidence; autonomy emerging. Makes decisions and has control of some aspects of life. Able to achieve some limited social integration/educational activities. Diffident over control over life. Needs encouragement to achieve potential.
4 Mostly confident; occasional difficulties integrating or in fulfilling social/role activity. Participating in all appropriate decisions. May have difficulty in achieving potential in some situations occasionally.
5 Achieving potential. Autonomous and unrestricted. Able to fulfil social, educational and family role.

WELL-BEING/DISTRESS

0 **Severe constant:** High and constant levels of distress/upset/concern/frustration/anger/distress/embarrassment/withdrawal/severe depression or apathy, unable to express or control emotions appropriately.
1 **Frequently severe:** Moderate distress/upset/concern/frustration/anger/distress/embarrassment/withdrawal/severe depression or apathy. Becomes concerned easily, requires constant reassurance/support, needs clear/tight limits and structure, loses emotional control easily.
2 **Moderate consistent:** Distress/upset/concern/frustration/anger/distress/embarrassment/withdrawal/severe depression or apathy in unfamiliar situations, frequent emotional encouragement and support required.
3 **Moderate frequent:** Distress/upset/concern/frustration/anger/distress/embarrassment/withdrawal/severe depression or apathy. Controls emotions with assistance, emotionally dependent on some occasions, vulnerable to change in routine, etc., spontaneously uses methods to assist emotional control.
4 **Mild occasional:** Distress/upset/concern/frustration/anger/distress/embarrassment/withdrawal/severe depression or apathy. Able to control feelings in most situations, generally well adjusted/stable (most of the time/most situations), occasional emotional support/encouragement needed.
5 **Not inappropriate:** Distress/upset/concern/frustration/anger/distress/embarrassment/withdrawal/severe depression or apathy. Well adjusted, stable and able to cope emotionally with most situations, good insight, accepts and understands own limitations.

20. MUSCULO-SKELETAL

Identify descriptor that is "best fit". The patient/client does not have to have each feature mentioned. Use 0.5 to indicate if patient/client is slightly better or worse than a descriptor and as appropriate to age.

IMPAIRMENT

0 Crippling, chronic, severe non-reversible deformity, severe inhibiting pain in several joints/parts of body. Severely limited range of movement and muscle power.
1 Severely restricted range of movement, partially reversible deformity, constant inhibiting pain/abnormal tone.
2 Moderate reversible deformity, restricted range of movement, redeemable muscle damage, inhibiting pain causing altered movement, moderate increased or decreased muscle tone. Poor exercise tolerance.
3 Correctable/slight deformity/slight increase or decrease muscle tone, 60% range of movement and muscle power. Intermittent pain resulting in occasional altered practice. Some inhibiting pain. Moderate exercise tolerance.
4 Slightly reduced muscle power, 80% range of movement, good exercise tolerance. Occasional discomfort.
5 Full range of movement and power. No pain, no abnormal muscle tone.

ACTIVITY

0 Immobile, totally dependent in all/any environments. Unable to participate in tasks.
1 Can transfer with maximal skilled physical assistance. Requires maximal assistance with all personal activities of daily living.
2 Requires regular assistance with activities of daily living can undertake some tasks independently.
3 Personal activities of daily living/transfers requiring supervision and some occasional help from carer.
4 Independent in adapted environment, needs occasional assistance or extra time with complex or unfamiliar activities.
5 Age-appropriate independent in all environments.

PARTICIPATION

0 Unable to fulfil any social/educational/family role. Not involved in decision-making/no autonomy/no control over environment; no social integration.
1 Low self-confidence/poor self-esteem/limited social integration/socially isolated/contributes to some basic and limited decisions. Cannot achieve potential in any situation.
2 Some self-confidence/some social integration/makes some decisions and influences control in familiar situations.
3 Some self-confidence; autonomy emerging. Makes decisions and has control of some aspects of life. Able to achieve some limited social integration/educational activities. Diffident over control over life. Needs encouragement to achieve potential.
4 Mostly confident; occasional difficulties integrating or in fulfilling social/role activity. Participating in all appropriate decisions. May have difficulty in achieving potential in some situations occasionally.
5 Achieving potential. Autonomous and unrestricted. Able to fulfil social, educational and family role.

WELL-BEING/DISTRESS

0 **Severe constant:** upset/frustration/anger/distress/embarrassment/concern/withdrawal. High and constant levels of concern/anger/severe depression or apathy, unable to express or control emotions appropriately.
1 **Frequently severe:** upset/frustration/anger/distress/embarrassment/concern/withdrawal. Moderate concern, becomes concerned easily, requires constant reassurance/support, needs clear/tight limits and structure, loses emotional control easily.
2 **Moderate consistent:** upset/frustration/anger/distress/embarrassment/concern/withdrawal. Concern in unfamiliar situation, frequent emotional encouragement and support required.
3 **Moderate frequent:** upset/frustration/anger/distress/embarrassment/concern/withdrawal. Controls emotions with assistance, emotionally dependent on some occasions, vulnerable to change in routine etc., spontaneously uses methods to assist emotional control.
4 **Mild occasional:** upset/frustration/anger/distress/embarrassment/concern/withdrawal. Able to control feelings in most situations, generally well adjusted/stable (most of the time/most situations), occasional emotional support/encouragement needed.
5 **Not inappropriate:** upset/frustration/anger/distress/embarrassment/concern/withdrawal.

21. RESPIRATORY CARE CHRONIC OBSTRUCTIVE PULMONARY DISEASE (COPD)

Identify descriptor that is "best fit". The patient/client does not have to have each feature mentioned. Use 0.5 to indicate if patient/client is slightly better or worse than a descriptor and as appropriate to age.

IMPAIRMENT

0 Full ventilatory support.

1 Some ventilatory support required, for example, night-time. Retains secretions/airway obstruction or altered air blood gases.

2 Requiring regular oxygen therapy/medication. Altered use of respiratory muscles. Help required to clear secretions. Altered air blood gases.

3 Lung function maintained with regular medication. Frequently normal air blood gases. Frequent productive cough, occasional problem with self-clearing of secretions

4 Normal lung function maintained with minimum medication. Non-problematic self-clearing of secretions. Normal air blood gases.

5 Normal lung function.

ACTIVITY

0 Unable to move, breathlessness at rest. Total care required (room bound).

1 Severe breathlessness on movement in bed, severe orthopnea, breathlessness affecting fluency of speech, requires maximal help in all activities (house bound).

2 Severe breathlessness on minimal exertion, i.e. transfer from bed to chair, any effort affects speech, can undertake a few ADL tasks unaided (house/immediate environment bound).

3 Breathlessness on walking on level ground – 50 yards. Normal speech when undertaking light activity. Independent for limited activities (access to local environment).

4 Breathlessness on flight of stairs, not breathless on level ground. Occasional reduction in complex or demanding tasks due to pain/breathlessness.

5 No functional disability, able to tackle exertion appropriate to age without respiratory distress.

PARTICIPATION

0 Unable to fulfil any social/educational/family role. Not involved in decision-making/no autonomy/no control over environment; no social integration.
1 Low self-confidence/poor self-esteem/limited social integration/socially isolated/contributes to some basic and limited decisions. Cannot achieve potential in any situation.
2 Some self-confidence/some social integration/makes some decisions and influences control in familiar situations.
3 Some self-confidence; autonomy emerging. Makes decisions and has control of some aspects of life. Able to achieve some limited social integration/educational activities. Diffident over control over life. Needs encouragement to achieve potential.
4 Mostly confident; occasional difficulties integrating or in fulfilling social/role activity. Participating in all appropriate decisions. May have difficulty in achieving potential in some situations occasionally.
5 Achieving potential. Autonomous and unrestricted. Able to fulfil social, educational and family role.

WELL-BEING/DISTRESS

0 **Severe constant:** upset/frustration/anger/distress/embarrassment/concern/withdrawal. High and constant levels of concern/anger/severe depression or apathy, unable to express or control emotions appropriately.
1 **Frequently severe:** upset/frustration/anger/distress/embarrassment/concern/withdrawal. Moderate concern, becomes concerned easily, requires constant reassurance/support, needs clear/tight limits and structure, loses emotional control easily.
2 **Moderate consistent:** upset/frustration/anger/distress/embarrassment/concern/withdrawal. Concern in unfamiliar situation, frequent emotional encouragement and support required.
3 **Moderate frequent:** upset/frustration/anger/distress/embarrassment/concern/withdrawal. Controls emotions with assistance, emotionally dependent on some occasions, vulnerable to change in routine etc., spontaneously uses methods to assist emotional control.
4 **Mild occasional:** upset/frustration/anger/distress/embarrassment/concern/withdrawal. Able to control feelings in most situations, generally well adjusted/stable (most of the time/most situations), occasional emotional support/encouragement needed.
5 **Not inappropriate:** upset/frustration/anger/distress/embarrassment/concern/withdrawal.

22. INCONTINENCE

Identify descriptor that is "best fit". The patient/client does not have to have each feature mentioned. Use 0.5 to indicate if patient/client is slightly better or worse than a descriptor and as appropriate to age.

IMPAIRMENT

0 No muscle power; bladder/bowel instability; no sensation, severe bladder/bowel prolapse; severe continual pain.
1 Flicker of muscle contraction. Intermittent severe pain.
2 Weak muscle contraction/diminished sensation. Some moderate pain.
3 Muscle contraction but not maintained against gravity. Evidence of instability. Occasional pain.
4 Muscle contraction against gravity. No pain; minor degree of prolapse.
5 Full muscle power and tone/stable bladder and bowel; full sensation, no prolapse.

ACTIVITY

0 Total lack of voluntary control; inability to recognise the need for bowel/bladder evacuation. Constant use of pads.
1 Recognising need to evacuate but inability to control.
2 Some ability to control bowel/bladder/frequency/urgency; only manages with structured routine, ability to go out for short periods with pads/toilet availability.
3 Intermittent bowel problems/frequent stress incontinence/urgency.
4 Very occasional stress incontinence.
5 Full bladder and bowel control.

PARTICIPATION

0 Unable to fulfil any social/educational/family role. Not involved in decision-making/no autonomy/no control over environment; no social integration.
1 Low self-confidence/poor self-esteem/limited social integration/socially isolated/contributes to some basic and limited decisions. Cannot achieve potential in any situation.
2 Some self-confidence/some social integration/makes some decisions and influences control in familiar situations.
3 Some self-confidence; autonomy emerging. Makes decisions and has control of some aspects of life. Able to achieve some limited social integration/educational activities. Diffident over control over life. Needs encouragement to achieve potential.
4 Mostly confident; occasional difficulties integrating or in fulfilling social/role activity. Participating in all appropriate decisions. May have difficulty in achieving potential in some situations occasionally.
5 Achieving potential. Autonomous and unrestricted. Able to fulfil social, educational and family role.

WELL-BEING/DISTRESS

0 **Severe constant:** upset/frustration/anger/distress/embarrassment/concern/withdrawal. High and constant levels of concern/anger/severe depression or apathy, unable to express or control emotions appropriately.
1 **Frequently severe:** upset/frustration/anger/distress/embarrassment/concern/withdrawal. Moderate concern, becomes concerned easily, requires constant reassurance/support, needs clear/tight limits and structure, loses emotional control easily.
2 **Moderate consistent:** upset/frustration/anger/distress/embarrassment/concern/withdrawal. Concern in unfamiliar situation, frequent emotional encouragement and support required.
3 **Moderate frequent:** upset/frustration/anger/distress/embarrassment/concern/withdrawal. Controls emotions with assistance, emotionally dependent on some occasions, vulnerable to change in routine etc., spontaneously uses methods to assist emotional control.
4 **Mild occasional:** upset/frustration/anger/distress/embarrassment/concern/withdrawal. Able to control feelings in most situations, generally well adjusted/stable (most of the time/most situations), occasional emotional support/encouragement needed.
5 **Not inappropriate:** upset/frustration/anger/distress/embarrassment/concern/withdrawal.

23. WOUND CARE

Identify descriptor that is "best fit". The patient/client does not have to have each feature mentioned. Use 0.5 to indicate if patient/client is slightly better or worse than a descriptor and as appropriate to age.

IMPAIRMENT

0 Black/necrotic full thickness wound or large surface area wound, for example, burn or large fungating wound with involvement of major blood vessels. Severe continual pain.

1 Deep wound extending to muscle, infected and inflamed or medium surface area wound. Severe pain, some relief with medication.

2 Sloughy wound, subcutaneous damage. Medium exudate, offensive smell. Moderate pain or occasional severe pain, relieved with medication.

3 Granulating clean wound. Epidermal damage, blistered, moist. Pain well controlled.

4 Superficial skin break. Inflamed, reddened area. Occasional discomfort.

5 Skin intact, healthy and pink.

ACTIVITY

0 Bed bound, semi-conscious. Totally dependent.

1 Bed/chair bound, requires maximum assistance with tasks but cooperates.

2 Chair bound, limited mobility, requires frequent assistance of one person. Can undertake some tasks independently.

3 Mobile with minimum assistance/supervision, requires some nursing intervention.

4 Can live independently. Mainly self-caring with occasional monitoring by other.

5 Totally independent and able to function normally.

PARTICIPATION

0 Unable to fulfil any social/educational/family role. Not involved in decision-making/no autonomy/no control over environment; no social integration.

1 Low self-confidence/poor self-esteem/limited social integration/socially isolated/contributes to some basic and limited decisions. Cannot achieve potential in any situation.

2 Some self-confidence/some social integration/makes some decisions and influences control in familiar situations.

3 Some self-confidence; autonomy emerging. Makes decisions and has control of some aspects of life. Able to achieve some limited social integration/educational activities. Diffident over control over life. Needs encouragement to achieve potential.

4 Mostly confident; occasional difficulties integrating or in fulfilling social/role activity. Participating in all appropriate decisions. May have difficulty in achieving potential in some situations occasionally.

5 Achieving potential. Autonomous and unrestricted. Able to fulfil social, educational and family role.

WELL-BEING/DISTRESS

0 **Severe constant:** upset/frustration/anger/distress/embarrassment/concern/withdrawal. High and constant levels of concern/anger/severe depression or apathy, unable to express or control emotions appropriately.

1 **Frequently severe:** upset/frustration/anger/distress/embarrassment/concern/withdrawal. Moderate concern, becomes concerned easily, requires constant reassurance/support, needs clear/tight limits and structure, loses emotional control easily.

2 **Moderate consistent:** upset/frustration/anger/distress/embarrassment/concern/withdrawal. Concern in unfamiliar situation, frequent emotional encouragement and support required.

3 **Moderate frequent:** upset/frustration/anger/distress/embarrassment/concern/withdrawal. Controls emotions with assistance, emotionally dependent on some occasions, vulnerable to change in routine etc., spontaneously uses methods to assist emotional control.

4 **Mild occasional:** upset/frustration/anger/distress/embarrassment/concern/withdrawal. Able to control feelings in most situations, generally well adjusted/stable (most of the time/most situations), occasional emotional support/encouragement needed.

5 **Not inappropriate:** upset/frustration/anger/distress/embarrassment/concern/withdrawal.

24. MENTAL HEALTH

Identify descriptor that is "best fit". The patient/client does not have to have each feature mentioned. Use 0.5 to indicate if patient/client is slightly better or worse than a descriptor and as appropriate to age.

IMPAIRMENT

0 Catatonic, unresponsive; no volition, persistent/severe and wide range of thought disorders, fixed delusions, persistent visual, auditory, tactile hallucinations, persistent/severe disturbance of affect. Severe memory loss. No insight.

1 Severe thought disorder, auditory hallucinations frequent, variable disturbances of affect, little volition. Occasionally past memories recalled. Some automatic response. Apathetic, no motivation, no initiation. Recognises own name and that of some individuals and situations. No insight into confusion.

2 Moderate thought disorder in duration, severity, frequency, some auditory hallucinations present, moderate disturbance of affect, moderate level of volition, some remote memory. Inappropriate responses to some stimuli. Occasional partial insight.

3 Evidence of some thought disorder, occasional evidence of auditory/visual hallucination, usually stable mood, volition intact. Some recent memory. Some insight. Attempting to express feeling and "sort things out". Orientated in regular surroundings, easily confused.

4 Very occasional evidence of some thought disorder in duration, severity, frequency, good level insight, usually stable mood, volition intact. Occasionally disturbed by new or occasional complex experiences. Short-term memory deficit. Can express feeling. Very occasional disorientation.

5 Well developed insight, high-level volition, no evidence of thought disorder, delusion, hallucination. Appropriate memory. Orientated.

ACTIVITY

0 Inability to recognise body functions and requirement. May have totally disruptive and uncooperative behaviour. Totally dependent, requires full physical care and constant vigilant supervision.

1 Recognises some bodily requirements and occasionally initiates actively but requires high level of assistance and supervision in most tasks.

2 Able to cooperate in self care and relate to others in protected environment but is dependent on verbal prompting to initiate and continue tasks. Requires some physical assistance.

3 Needs occasional verbal prompting to initiate movement/care/able to operate without supervision for short periods, able to have some independence with encouragement. Independent in familiar surroundings only.

4 Able to live independently with some occasional support, requires extra time, encouragement. Assistance occasionally required with unfamiliar tasks.

5 Age-appropriate independence.

PARTICIPATION

0 Unable to fulfil any social/educational/family role. Not involved in decision-making/no autonomy/no control over environment; no social integration.
1 Low self-confidence/poor self-esteem/limited social integration/socially isolated/contributes to some basic and limited decisions. Cannot achieve potential in any situation.
2 Some self-confidence/some social integration/makes some decisions and influences control in familiar situations.
3 Some self-confidence; autonomy emerging. Makes decisions and has control of some aspects of life. Able to achieve some limited social integration/educational activities. Diffident over control over life. Needs encouragement to achieve potential.
4 Mostly confident; occasional difficulties integrating or in fulfilling social/role activity. Participating in all appropriate decisions. May have difficulty in achieving potential in some situations occasionally.
5 Achieving potential. Autonomous and unrestricted. Able to fulfil social, educational and family role.

WELL-BEING/DISTRESS

0 **Severe constant:** upset/frustration/anger/distress/embarrassment/concern/withdrawal. High and constant levels of concern/anger/severe depression or apathy, unable to express or control emotions appropriately.
1 **Frequently severe:** upset/frustration/anger/distress/embarrassment/concern/withdrawal. Moderate concern, becomes concerned easily, requires constant reassurance/support, needs clear/tight limits and structure, loses emotional control easily.
2 **Moderate consistent:** upset/frustration/anger/distress/embarrassment/concern/withdrawal. Concern in unfamiliar situation, frequent emotional encouragement and support required.
3 **Moderate frequent:** upset/frustration/anger/distress/embarrassment/concern/withdrawal. Controls emotions with assistance, emotionally dependent on some occasions, vulnerable to change in routine etc., spontaneously uses methods to assist emotional control.
4 **Mild occasional:** upset/frustration/anger/distress/embarrassment/concern/withdrawal. Able to control feelings in most situations, generally well adjusted/stable (most of the time/most situations), occasional emotional support/encouragement needed.
5 **Not inappropriate:** upset/frustration/anger/distress/embarrassment/concern/withdrawal.

25. MENTAL HEALTH – ANXIETY

Identify descriptor that is "best fit". The patient/client does not have to have each feature mentioned. Use 0.5 to indicate if patient/client is slightly better or worse than a descriptor and as appropriate to age.

IMPAIRMENT

0 Continual demonstration of global severe symptoms with no relief.

1 Severe anxiety/stress symptoms demonstrated most of the time but sometimes/circumstances where partial relief is experienced.

2 Some situations/times when anxiety/stress is severe or moderate anxiety/stress frequently experienced (daily) but there are periods when anxiety is not a problem.

3 Anxiety/stress occasionally severe (weekly) can manage stress on some occasions but may need prompting and support with strategies.

4 Anxiety/stress levels easily aroused but copes when strategies in place, very occasional difficulties.

5 Normal response in stressful situations.

ACTIVITY

0 Physically dependent for all functional tasks. No self care skills

1 Dependent for most tasks but will cooperate. Physical assistance required frequently. Carer undertaking burden of tasks.

2 Most tasks, needs verbal and physical prompts to initiate.

3 Some physical/verbal support and encouragement to complete some tasks but initiates appropriately.

4 Occasional verbal encouragement needed and support or extra time required for specific tasks.

5 Independent in all areas.

PARTICIPATION

0 Unable to fulfil any social/educational/family role. Not involved in decision-making/no autonomy/no control over environment; no social integration.

1 Low self-confidence/poor self-esteem/limited social integration/socially isolated/contributes to some basic and limited decisions. Cannot achieve potential in any situation.

2 Some self-confidence/some social integration/makes some decisions and influences control in familiar situations.

3 Some self-confidence; autonomy emerging. Makes decisions and has control of some aspects of life. Able to achieve some limited social integration/educational activities. Diffident over control over life. Needs encouragement to achieve potential.

4 Mostly confident; occasional difficulties integrating or in fulfilling social/role activity. Participating in all appropriate decisions. May have difficulty in achieving potential in some situations occasionally.

5 Achieving potential. Autonomous and unrestricted. Able to fulfil social, educational and family role.

WELL-BEING/DISTRESS

0 **Severe constant:** upset/frustration/anger/distress/embarrassment/concern/withdrawal. High and constant levels of concern/anger/severe depression or apathy, unable to express or control emotions appropriately.

1 **Frequently severe:** upset/frustration/anger/distress/embarrassment/concern/withdrawal. Moderate concern, becomes concerned easily, requires constant reassurance/support, needs clear/tight limits and structure, loses emotional control easily.

2 **Moderate consistent:** upset/frustration/anger/distress/embarrassment/concern/withdrawal. Concern in unfamiliar situation, frequent emotional encouragement and support required.

3 **Moderate frequent:** upset/frustration/anger/distress/embarrassment/concern/withdrawal. Controls emotions with assistance, emotionally dependent on some occasions, vulnerable to change in routine etc., spontaneously uses methods to assist emotional control.

4 **Mild occasional:** upset/frustration/anger/distress/embarrassment/concern/withdrawal. Able to control feelings in most situations, generally well adjusted/stable (most of the time/most situations), occasional emotional support/encouragement needed.

5 **Not inappropriate:** upset/frustration/anger/distress/embarrassment/concern/withdrawal.

26. SCHIZOPHRENIA

Identify descriptor that is "best fit". The patient/client does not have to have each feature mentioned. Use 0.5 to indicate if patient/client is slightly better or worse than a descriptor and as appropriate to age.

IMPAIRMENT

0 No insight, no volition, persistent/severe and wide range of thought disorder, fixed delusions, persistent visual, auditory, tactile hallucinations, persistent/severe disturbance of affect. Severe emotional blunting. Absence of empathy.

1 Thought disorder with variability, auditory hallucinations frequent, variable disturbance of affect, little volition. Severe-moderate emotional blunting. Very occasional empathy present.

2 Moderate thought disorder in duration, severity, frequency, some auditory hallucinations present, moderate disturbance of affect, moderate level of volition. Moderate emotional blunting. Empathy present to a limited extent.

3 Occasional evidence of though disorder in duration, severity, frequency, very occasional evidence of auditory hallucination, usually stable mood, volition intact. Occasional/mild emotional blunting. Appropriate empathy on occasions.

4 Very occasional evidence of some thought disorder in duration, severity, frequency, good level insight, usually stable mood, volition intact. No emotional blunting, appropriate empathy.

5 Well developed insight, high level of volition, no evidence of thought disorder, delusion, hallucinations, consistently stable mood.

ACTIVITY

0 Physically dependent for all functional tasks, bed/chair bound, no self care skills, inability to communicate, no attention.

1 Dependent for most tasks but will cooperate/assist with maximal prompting, needs cues and reminders for activities of daily living, occasional small amount of verbal communication with individual members of staff. No insight.

2 Able to initiate some aspects of activities of daily living, for example, dressing. Understandable communication increased with some meaningful content, able to concentrate for a short time, easily distracted. Needs frequent supervision and prompting. Occasional insight.

3 Some consistency in communication, for example, interacting with staff/carers and other clients, able to initiate a broader range of activities of daily living, responding to demands of rehabilitation.

4 Minimal assistance needed in less familiar environments, communicating effectively with a wide range of groups and individuals, concentrating on a majority of necessary activities. Uses self-help prompts well. Good insight.

5 Independent, no assistance needed for ADL, communicating effectively with a wide range of groups and individuals, concentrates on all necessary activities.

PARTICIPATION

0 Unable to fulfil any social/educational/family role. Not involved in decision-making/no autonomy/no control over environment; no social integration.

1 Low self-confidence/poor self-esteem/limited social integration/socially isolated/contributes to some basic and limited decisions. Cannot achieve potential in any situation.

2 Some self-confidence/some social integration/makes some decisions and influences control in familiar situations.

3 Some self-confidence; autonomy emerging. Makes decisions and has control of some aspects of life. Able to achieve some limited social integration/educational activities. Diffident over control over life. Needs encouragement to achieve potential.

4 Mostly confident; occasional difficulties integrating or in fulfilling social/role activity. Participating in all appropriate decisions. May have difficulty in achieving potential in some situations occasionally.

5 Achieving potential. Autonomous and unrestricted. Able to fulfil social, educational and family role.

WELL-BEING/DISTRESS

0 **Severe constant:** upset/frustration/anger/distress/embarrassment/concern/withdrawal. High and constant levels of concern/anger/severe depression or apathy, unable to express or control emotions appropriately.

1 **Frequently severe:** upset/frustration/anger/distress/embarrassment/concern/withdrawal. Moderate concern, becomes concerned easily, requires constant reassurance/support, needs clear/tight limits and structure, loses emotional control easily.

2 **Moderate consistent:** upset/frustration/anger/distress/embarrassment/concern/withdrawal. Concern in unfamiliar situation, frequent emotional encouragement and support required.

3 **Moderate frequent:** upset/frustration/anger/distress/embarrassment/concern/withdrawal. Controls emotions with assistance, emotionally dependent on some occasions, vulnerable to change in routine etc., spontaneously uses methods to assist emotional control.

4 **Mild occasional:** upset/frustration/anger/distress/embarrassment/concern/withdrawal. Able to control feelings in most situations, generally well adjusted/stable (most of the time/most situations), occasional emotional support/encouragement needed.

5 **Not inappropriate:** upset/frustration/anger/distress/embarrassment/concern/withdrawal.

APPENDIX VIII
ADAPTED TOM SCALES IN DEVELOPMENT

26. AUGMENTATIVE COMMUNICATION

(Developed by Frenchay Speech and Language Therapy department, March 1994)

IMPAIRMENT – RELATED TO STATED COMMUNICATION DISORDER (e.g. dysarthria, dysgraphia)

0 Severe level of communication impairment.
1 Severe/moderate level of communication impairment. Some variability.
2 Moderate communication impairment.
3 Moderate to slight communication impairment.
4 Slight level of communication impairment.
5 No communication impairment.

ACTIVITY

0 No functional communication in any mode. Unable to respond to auditory, visual or sensory stimulation.
1 Very occasional communication, using some purposeful responses to indicate limited needs or feelings, with informed immediate carers.
2 Some functional communication with trained listeners. Reliable Yes/No response. Consistent attempts at purposeful communication. Speech, reading and writing is non-functional for communication purposes.
3 Consistent level of functional communication with trained listeners. Some limitations to output related to restricted access to symbol set, spelling or reading, resulting in a limited vocabulary.
4 Functional communication available to the individual in most circumstances through any selected communication mode with sympathetic listeners. Speech/voice weak and requiring augmentation. Some communication modes inaccessible to the individuals, for example telephone. Access to extensive vocabulary.
5 Able to communicate to anyone in any circumstances using all communication modes.

27. COMMUNICATION EFFECTIVENESS

(Developed by West Birmingham Speech and Language Therapy Service)

IMPAIRMENT

0 The most severe presentation of this impairment

1 Severe presentation of this impairment

2 Severe/moderate presentation

3 Moderate presentation

4 Just below normal/mild presentation

5 No impairment

ACTIVITY – COMMUNICATION

0 Functioning at pre-intentional level.

1 Limited functional communication, only communicates about items within immediate reach or view.

2 Use of speech signs or symbols to communicate basic needs information to familiar people.

3 Use of speech signs or symbols to transfer specific information to familiar people when the context is known.

4 Use of speech signs and symbols to transfer specific information when the context is not known. Able to transfer basic information to new people.

5 Transfers information to new people and able to give specific information about a range of topics.

28. ENVIRONMENTAL AIDS

ACTIVITY – PERFORMANCE

0 Cannot perform activity even with aid/s.

1 Able to perform limited activities only with aid/s. This includes activity with others, such as, adjusting or controlling environment.

2 Able to perform a range of activities through use of aid/s. Depends on others for help with some activities.

3 Able to perform some activities unaided and on own with difficulty. Able to perform a range of activities through use of aid/s independently, though help is needed for some activities.

4 Able to perform most activities on own without difficulty.

5 Able to perform activities independently.

APPENDIX IX
CLASSIFICATION OF DISORDERS – ICD-10

The Therapy Outcome Measure (TOM) can provide information on the change of an individual patient or, if coded in a consistent fashion, it can be aggregated to provide information on groups of patients. Such aggregation, particularly if it is to be used for comparisons or benchmarking, relies on accurate coding of the patient groups.

In this version of the TOM, we recommend the use of the International Statistical Classification of Diseases and Health Related Problems (10th Edition) (ICD-10) published by the World Health Organisation (WHO). This system of classification is commonly used in the management of health provision and allows the classification of diseases, which are defined as a system of categories to which morbid entities are assigned according to established criteria. The purpose of the ICD is to "permit the systematic recording, analysis, interpretation and comparison of mortality and morbidity data collected in different countries or areas and at different times". It is used to translate diagnoses of diseases and other health problems from words into alphanumeric codes, which permit easy storage, retrieval and analysis of the data. This classification has become the international standard for all general epidemiological and health management purposes, which can include the analysis of the general health situation of population groups, monitoring of incidence and prevalence of disease, audit, research and basic monitoring.

The ICD-10 codes can be used to represent diseases and other health problems recorded on many types of health and other records. We provide an abridged list of codes, which may be frequently used by therapists. Therapists may, however, wish to add to these, particularly if they are working in specialist units or require more precision in their coding. For example we provide the code for cleft palate as "Q35". If a particular therapist wishes to identify different clients in this category with more precision they may refer to the full classification and they will find that Q35.0 is the code for cleft hard palate, bilateral; Q35.1 is the code for cleft hard palate, unilateral; Q35.2 is cleft soft palate bilateral and Q35.3 is cleft soft palate unilateral. A further example of interest to physiotherapists and occupational therapists is related to amputation. The full ICD-10 listing provides numerous codes for the type, level and cause of amputation, which may be of interest and importance to specialist units. In our abstracted version below, we have only included "acquired absence of limb surgical or traumatic" Z89 and congenital absence of limb Q71. The full version provides codes for "acquired absence of hand and wrist"

Z89.1. "Acquired absence of foot and ankle" Z89.4, etc. Space limits our abridged version

Users of the system must be attentive to accuracy. Thus, a code with three letters e.g., Q37, should not add a third digit, e.g., a "0" to this as this will change the meaning of the term from cleft palate with cleft lip (Q37) to cleft hard palate with cleft lip, bilateral (Q37.0).

Communication and Swallowing	
Disorders of Fluency	F98.5
Cluttering	F98.6
Dysphonia (Organic)	R49.0
Psychogenic voice disorder	R44.4
Laryngitis	J04.0
Neoplasm of Larynx	D38
Aphasia/Dysphasia	R47.0
Progressive dysphasia	G31.0
Dyslexia	R48.0
Dysarthria and Anarthria	R47.1
Dyspraxia	R48.2
Dysphagia	R13
Autistic Communication Disorder	F84.0
Aspergers Syndrome	F84.5
Specific Developmental Disorders of Language	F80
Semantic/Pragmatic Disorder	F80.1
Developmental Language Impairment	F80.9
Development Articulation Impairment	F80.0
Hearing Loss	H90

Cleft Palate	Q35
Cleft Palate with cleft lip	Q37
General Learning Disability	F79
Behavioural	F91.9
Hypernasality/Hyponasality	R49.2
Schizophrenia	F20
Eating disorder Behavioural (not dysphagia)	F50
Respiratory Disease	
Acute Bronchitis	J20
Chronic Bronchitis	J42
Viral pneumonia	J12
Bacterial pneumonia	J15
Pneumonia not specified	J18
Bronchitis not specified	J40
Asthma	J45
Other Respiratory disorders	J98
Emphysema	J43
Chronic obstructive pulmonary disease	J44
Obstetrics and Gynaecology	
Endometriosis	N80
Female Genital prolapse	N81
Post procedural disorders of genitourinary system (e.g. post surgery or radiation)	N99

Long Labour	O63
Stress incontinence	N39.3
Unspecified urinary incontinence	R32
Back Disorders	
Scoliosis unspecified	M41.9
Spinal osteoporosis unspecified	M2.9
Torticollis	M43.6
Spondylosis unspecified	M47.9
Cervical disc disorder	M50
Intervertebral disc disorder	M51
Sciatica	M54.3
Low back pain	M54.5
Musculo skeletal	
Juvenile Arthritis	M08
Rheumatoid Arthritis	M06
Osteoarthritis – Polyarthrosis	M15
Arthrosis of hip	M16
Arthrosis of knee	M17
Other Arthrosis	M19
Other joint disorder (excluding back)	M25
Systemic connective tissue disorder	M35
Disorder of muscle – unspecified	M62.9

Orthopaedic	
Fracture ribs, sternum, thoracic spine	S22
Fracture lumbar spine/pelvis	S32
Fracture shoulder/upper arm	S42
Fracture forearm	S52
Dislocation/sprain of joints/ligaments of neck	S13
Dislocation/sprain of joints/ligaments lumbar spine/pelvic	S33
Dislocation/sprain of joints/ligaments shoulder girdle	S43
Dislocation/sprain of joints/ligaments elbow	S53
Dislocation/sprain of joints/ligaments hip	S73
Dislocation/sprain of joints/ligaments knee	S83
Dislocation/sprain of joints/ligaments ankle/foot	S93
Fracture femur	S72
Fracture lower leg/ankle	S82
Amputation	
Acquired absence of limb surgical or traumatic	Z89
Congenital absence of upper limb	Q71
Congenital absence of lower limb	Q72
Mental Illness	
Dementia in Alzheimer's Disease	F00
Unspecified dementia	F03
Organic personality disorder	F07.0
Schizophrenia	F20
Acute and transient psychotic disorders	F23

Bipolar affective disorder	F31
Depression	F32
Phobic anxiety disorder	F40
Obsessive Compulsive Disorder	F42
Eating disorder (not dysphagia)	F50
Unspecified mental disorder of adult personality and behaviour	F69
Diseases of Circulatory System	
Chronic ischemic heart disease	I25
Acute myocardial infarction	I21
Angina	I20
Pulmonary embolism	I26
Endocarditis	I33
Cardiac arrest	I46
Heart Failure	I50
Cerebrovascular Diseases	
Subarachnoid haemorrhage	I60
Intra cerebral haemorrhage	I61
Cerebral Infarction	I63
Stroke not specified	I64
Other cerebrovascular disease	I67
Diseases of nervous system	
Huntington's disease	G10
Systemic nervous system atrophies	G13

Parkinson's Disease	G20
Other degenerative disease of basal ganglia	G23
Dystonia	G24
Other extra-pyramidal and movement	G25
Epilepsy	G40
Facial nerve disorders	G51
Transient cerebral ischemic attack	G45
Myasthenia syndromes	G73
Infantile cerebral palsy	G80
Multiple Sclerosis	G35
Motor Neurone disease	G12.2
Flaccid hemiplegia	G81.0
Spastic hemiplegia	G81.1
Unspecified hemiplegia	G81.9
Flaccid paraplegia	G82.0
Spastic paraplegia	G82.1
Unspecified paraplegia	G82.2
Other paralytic syndromes	G83
Developmental Conditions	
Delayed Development	R62.0
Developmental Disorder of motor function	F82
Mixed specific developmental disorder	F83
Mental Retardation (mild)	F70

Mental Retardation (moderate)	F71
Mental Retardation (severe)	F72
Specific developmental disorder scholastic achievement	F81
General Learning Disability	F79
Cerebral Palsy	G80
Pain	
Acute pain	R52.0
Chronic pain	R52.1
Head Injury	
Traumatic Cerebral edema	S06.1
Diffuse brain injury	S06.2
Focal brain injury	S06.3
Traumatic sub-dural haemorrhage	S06.5
Other	
Nothing abnormal detected	Z71.1
Burns	T30.0

Index

Note: Page numbers followed by *t* indicate by tables.